HOPE FOR WOUNDED WARRIORS

BY
LARRY J. WEBB

ADAPTED FROM
"MY STORY"
BY
BILL LENTSCH
(Marine Survivor - Guadalcanal 1942)

MW00905573

Hope For Wounded Warriors
Copyright 2012
By
Larry J. Webb

All rights reserved. No portion of this book may be reproduced, stored in a retrieval system, or transmitted in any form or by any means – electronic, mechanical, photocopy, recording, or any other – except for brief quotations in printed reviews, without the prior permission of the copyright holder.

Cover and errata updated December 2012

Scripture quotations are from The Holy Bible (KJV) or are the author's paraphrases.

Correspondence and inquires

should be directed to

Larry J. Webb

HopeforWoundedWarriors@gmail.com

ISBN-13: 978-1479140176

ISBN-10: 1479140171

DEDICATION

to

BILL LENTSCH

MARINE SURVIVOR
GUADALCANAL

Whose courage and faith have been and always will be – a source of inspiration to many ... and to future generations.

August 2012

ACKNOWLEDGEMENTS –

With deep gratitude to

CHAPLAIN PAUL SLATER - computer & technical assistance in the publishing process.

RANDY WEBB - cover photo of Bill Lentsch's Purple Heart

HOPE FOR WOUNDED WARRIORS

Table of Contents

AUTHOR'S / EDITOR'S PREFACE

As a wounded warrior, Bill Lentsch knows the frustrating feelings of apparent helplessness and hopelessness. A sea-going Marine on the cruiser USS Vincennes at the beginning of World War II, he was a "hot shell catcher".

In the heat of battle, to avoid the danger of fire on the wooden deck, personnel burns, and possible jamming of the swivel mechanism ... dressed with asbestos arm length gloves and apron, he caught the red hot empty shell casings as they were ejected from one of the 5 inch guns and tossed them overboard.

The USS Vincennes was part of the invasion fleet when our Marines landed on Guadalcanal in August 1942. The Japanese defenders responded by mounting a three day aerial attack. In the middle of the night, the Japanese Navy launched a sea attack upon the exhausted fleet. Before dawn the USS Vincennes would lie at the bottom of the sea.

The story of Bill's survival when the Vincennes sank is a story of miracles. In contrast, the story of his post-war rehabilitation and readjustment to civilian life, including a bad marriage, contains more than its share of dark pages and the consequences of poor choices. But the story of his later years brings hope and inspiration as Bill shares his personal journey of discovery.

From the vantage point of over ninety years ... even with eyes encrusted with cataracts, he can now "see" that God had a plan and a purpose for including Bill Lentsch among the survivors. I hope as you read that you will also be able to "see" a glimpse of the possibilities in store for every individual who will make a full surrender to God.

During his retirement years Bill recorded his story with a dictating machine in numerous different sessions. This resulted in an abundance of duplicate material and many long, run-on sentences.

In 2005, as a gift to my special friend, I transcribed those many hours of dictation, deleted redundancies, and attempted to reconcile any conflicting accounts. However, because it was Bill's Story ... spoken from his heart, I have chosen not to eliminate every grammatical error or instance of broken syntax. Hopefully it will permit the reader to "hear" the emotions of Bill's soul as he shared his journey.

The reader may already have noticed that this writer often uses 3 dots (...). Sometimes they take the place of a comma ... but always, it is an invitation to pause and think about it. Hopefully it will make the story more meaningful.

Five copies of that original manuscript were spiral bound under the title "MY STORY" By BILL LENTSCH (William Edmond Lentsch) Survivor U.S.S. Cruiser Vincennes Torpedoed Off Guadalcanal 1942 Transcribed from voice tapes and edited to remove redundancies by Larry J. Webb

Bill had hoped that Hallmark or some other producer might develop a screen play and make a film of it with proceeds going to a favorite charity. To date that has not transpired, but with the 70th anniversary of the battle for Guadalcanal upon us, and with the hundreds of wounded warriors sometimes facing those same feelings of apparent helplessness and hopelessness, with Bill's permission, I have done a rewrite ... adding historical information and orientation as well as eliminating some material and condensing as well as expanding other portions to sharpen the focus and facilitate its publication.

The end result is still Bill's "story" ... mostly in his words ... but adapted to a new purpose.

It is especially hoped that veterans, returning from the wars in Iraq and Afghanistan, as well as future veterans, might take courage and find hope in their personal journeys in life. Bill discovered that there is help ... and there is "HOPE FOR WOUNDED WARRIORS".

Larry J. Webb Hope4WoundedWarriors@gmail.com

CHAPTER 1: A MIRACLE SURVIVAL

In the early morning hours of August 9, 1942 the heavy cruiser USS Vincennes sank to a watery grave following three days of intense battle during the Marine assault on Guadalcanal. When the sun came up in the morning, only a remnant of that crew of over 1200 Sailors and Marines were among the survivors.

Many of them never made it home again. Large numbers succumbed to the trauma of their battle wounds and painful burns even if they were lucky enough to be found by rescue craft in those shark infested waters off the coast of Savo Island.

I was one of those fortunate few who were snatched from the jaws of death. Some may call it random chance. Others, lucky circumstances. But for me ... looking back over these almost 70 years, I see the awesome "fingerprints" of a gracious God. You be the judge, I'll just tell it like I saw it.

Not that I deserved any special treatment. I was a Marine ... and the names of Marines are not noted for inclusion in very many people's list of saints. And how a skinny kid from New Haven, Connecticut, ever made it into the Marines is another story ... but we'll save that for later. Right now, let's focus on the USS Vincennes.

After the infamous attack by the Japanese at Pearl Harbor on December 7, 1941, the USS Vincennes was shifted from escorting lend lease convoys in the North Atlantic to the Pacific theater. Her first assignment was to the flotilla of ships that escorted the aircraft carrier "Hornet" carrying Jimmy Doolittle and his bomber group to within striking distance of Tokyo for a daring retaliatory attack on 18 April 1942.

For people in their 80s and 90s ... these are vivid memories. For younger readers ... maybe we ought to digress for a few moments for some historic orientation. The names found on maps today are dramatically different from the names on our maps as kids in school.

The names on our maps revealed the arrogant realities of prideful national empires. We could locate the British West Indies, French Guiana, the Belgium Congo, the Dutch East Indies, and similarly named places. European countries, even tiny ones like Belgium and Holland, had wrested control of much of the world, exploiting and exporting the rich resources that they discovered.

The Japanese military and political leaders saw the expanding empires of the French in Vietnam, the Dutch in Indonesia, the British in India, and the U.S. in the Philippines ... and, as some historians postulate, they decided that, if the world was up for grabs, they would grab some too.

So they put their eyes on the mainland Asian countries of Korea, Mongolia, China, and the Pacific Islands including the oil-rich resources of Indonesia upon which their military machine depended. I say this, not to justify any of it, but simply to set the stage.

With the United States, not yet officially in a declared war with Germany, (but obviously deeply involved in helping the British to defend England), the Japanese made a pact with Hitler's Germany ... forming an "axis." By striking at Pearl Harbor they would involve the U.S. with a war in the Pacific, distracting us enough to allow Hitler to finally succeed in conquering both England and Russia.

Following that attack on Pearl Harbor, our strategy was to retake the scores of Pacific Islands ... denying to Japan the imported oil she needed to continue her conquests. We did it with heavy bombardments ... followed by Marines wading ashore to secure a beachhead ... and then landing Army units to push across the island, destroying the Japanese defenders hiding in caves and fortified defenses. The expansive cemeteries with their white crosses on each of those islands are testimony to the heavy cost involved.

In August 1942, next on our agenda to recapture those islands, was a place called Guadalcanal. It contained a major airfield, and its control was crucial to our success in the Pacific. Planes from our aircraft carriers had been bombing the place. At 05:00 hrs. on the morning of the invasion, we began to shell the beaches with what we called "star shells." They would light up the beaches as they were falling, and then explode on contact. (Pretty impressive!!!)

We worked in a rotation pattern. Sailing parallel to the beach, the guns on the starboard side would fire. Then the ship would circle around, and the guns from the port side would take their turn at the shelling.

Around 06:00 hrs., the landing craft were launched from the ships with us, and we watched as the Marines hit the beach amid stiff resistance. Meanwhile, we continued the bombardment further inland to try to keep the defenders pinned down. We circled around the Guadalcanal harbor along with the cruiser Quincy and the Australian cruiser Canberra, plus two other light cruisers, the Astoria and the Nashville.

My job was to catch the hot shell casings coming out of the breech of the five inch antiaircraft gun. Each time that a shell would be loaded into the gun, I would position myself so that I could receive the hot shell casing as it was ejected from the gun.

I had asbestos gloves on all the way up to my shoulder pits. They covered pretty much all the front of me. I would catch those white hot shell casings and toss them over the side into the ocean.

The reason for it was, if they were scattered on the deck, they could immobilize the gun so it couldn't swivel around to fire at the aircraft coming in from various directions. So my job was to be sure those shell casings did not remain on the deck although some would hit the deck because at times they were firing every few seconds and swiveling to follow the planes. I would grab them and toss them overboard.

This continued for three days ... with the Japanese air force attacking our ships with dive bombers, torpedoes, and kamikaze suicide planes. During this time we had no solid food.

The evening of August 8, it quieted down enough for our cooks, who had been completely occupied helping to man the guns, fight fires, and carry casualties, went to the kitchen and broke out stale bread, cans of peaches and whatever was available to feed the crew.

Then we dropped into our bunks exhausted. We didn't know where the Japanese Navy was ... but we knew that they had a famous strategy to attack with the "rising sun" ... so we wanted to be ready.

At 01:30 hrs. in the morning of August 9, 1942, the bugle sounded over the loud speaker system that we were being attacked. I had a pair of shorts on and I was transferred from the hot shell man position to move ammo from the storage areas because a number of men had been wounded and were in sickbay right beside the Marine compartment. (I understood later they were just kicking the shells out of the way as they came out of the breech of the gun.)

So they transferred me down to be one of the shell loaders. When the shells came up the hoist from the hold, we moved them onto our hoist in the Marine compartment and then pressed a button and they were automatically taken up to the gun.

We had watertight integrity ... doors that were bolted down to help the ship stay afloat in the event that we were hit. I hadn't been out of bed and onto my position more than a couple of minutes when a loud explosion took place ... and then another and another.

We didn't realize what was going on underneath us. Later I found out that we had taken three torpedoes. Suddenly a large shell came through the sick bay next door ... blew open the doors. I understand it killed the doctor and several of the corpsmen and patients that were there.

The explosion blew open the door into our compartment, and water started coming in through a hole on the waterline.   As it exploded, it threw me against the bulkhead. I wasn't hurt too badly, just kind of bruised. I picked myself up, shook myself, and noticed there were a couple of Sailors that were unconscious. I helped revive them and got them to a ladder. I told them the ship was going to be sinking, and they needed to get out. They started to climb up to the next deck.

Our hoist had gone dead because of the power going out, but there were still some shells in our compartment. There were no lights.   The water had started to come in through the side of the ship. The compartment was filling up slowly. I decided I wanted to stay a little longer and see if I couldn't get some more shells pushed up to the top by hand. I knew that as long as the gun crew had ammo, we could make a difference in the battle.

Suddenly a second shell hit our area. Water started gushing in and filling the compartment. This explosion picked me up, threw me around and slammed me against the bulkhead. My right leg was jammed up into my chest cavity and broken in eighteen places ... my spine twisted; I slumped back into the water. I was dazed ... teeth were knocked loose in my mouth ... and I began to pray.

My prayer was, "Oh God, save me!" I couldn't do anything. I couldn't walk. I couldn't move. I was partially paralyzed. The paint was burning on the ceiling and part of the bulkheads giving a little light like so many candles. I couldn't move under the weight of some of the lockers and bunks that had toppled over onto me. As the water began to come up around my neck, I yelled for help ... but it didn't seem like there was anyone there.

But God was watching over me. When the water got up to my nose, I knew it was just moments before I would drown ... when those same two Sailors that I had rescued earlier, jumped down off the ladder, pulled the wreckage off of me, and lifted me up and dragged me over to the ladder. They put my hands on the chains of the ladder and then disappeared up the ladder.

The ship lurched and was beginning to list over on its side. With my two arms I dragged myself up three decks to the top deck where I noticed that the commander's cabin had a huge hole in it.

As I lay there on the top deck, everything was ablaze including the hanger deck where our two observation planes were burning. The deck was all afire as it was a wooden deck. The paint was burning on the ship and the ship had about a 30 degree list. Gravely wounded, I had hot burning paint dropping onto my back. I had fourth degree burns, and I could barely move.

A Sailor came by and dragged me under a hose that was spewing salt water. It soothed my back some. I wondered how I was going to survive. As I lay there in that cooling spray, I could see the water advancing up the deck. The smoke was rising, and the steam was coming closer. I began to pray that God would somehow get me off this ship before it went down.

About that time, a man came by, a young fellow, a friend of mine who worked as a chaplain's assistant. He took off his life jacket, put it on me and said, "Don't worry, I can swim and I'll find a life raft to keep me afloat, or I can find another life jacket." Then he helped me roll under the life lines on the ship and slide into the water.

With my arms, I paddled my way out, away from the ship, realizing that if I remained too close, when it went under, the suction would take me with it. I was anxious to get away from the ship.

I had only gotten a few yards when the search lights from an enemy ship found me, and the machine guns started spraying the area. I felt a sting in my arm, so I played dead in the water. My face ... I would lift it up a little for bits of air and then go back under.

Eventually, when the enemy ship had steamed past and the area was no longer illuminated by their search light, I paddled away from the ship. The sharks were active, just tearing these wounded men apart. It was chaos there in the dark. Meanwhile, both the Quincy and the Canberra had been sunk ... and I could see that the Astoria had been run aground and was burning on the beach.

I watched as the Vincennes began to lurch and finally, as it started to go over, we could hear the last blast of the horn. I saw the Captain dive off the bridge into the water and disappear. The ship then, of course, went down. I understand today that National Geographic found the ship. It was sitting straight up the way it would normally sit if it was on the water, except it was sitting in quite a bit of mud five miles down off Guadalcanal.

By that time I realized that my chest was full ... I don't know why my heart was not punctured, but the Lord was there with me. I paddled around in the dark, splashing to keep the sharks away, knowing that blood oozing from my wounds would attract them.

Suddenly, I felt something bump me in the back. It was a life raft. On this life raft were two Sailors. They grabbed underneath my armpits and lifted me onto the raft. I was so badly swollen and the pain was so great ... every now and then I would pass out and then come to.

We drifted quite a few hours. One of the times I came to consciousness ... my best friend ... I saw the sharks take him away. He had lost both an arm and a leg.

Before we had picked up many other survivors on the raft, the Sailors that had rescued me recognized me. They said, "You're one of those guys that attended the Bible study in the chapel. We know you. You're a so-called Christian aren't you?"

I said, "Well, after a fashion." And they said, "Well, if there's a God in heaven, and you really believe that, you pray that it will rain right now." I said, "Come on, fellows. It doesn't rain in the South Pacific unless it's the season." I said, "The moon and the stars are out. There's no way." They said, "We're starving for water. Pray!"

In my simple faith I looked up and said, "Lord, let it rain." A big black thunder cloud came up, a clap of lightning, thunder, and the sky opened up and poured out rain for two or three minutes. They opened their mouths and I opened mine. We each got a mouthful of rain water ... and then the cloud went away ... but I'll never forget that answer to prayer.

As we drifted through the night we began to pick up survivors from the water. One that we picked up was the Captain of the ship. He had a mean gash across his back.

As the morning broke a destroyer came alongside. The commander hollered out through a megaphone: "Who is the highest in command on that raft?" The Captain responded, "I'm Captain Riefkohl. I'm the highest in command." So the commander of the destroyer said, "When we lower the cargo net, we want you to get in it and bring all the senior officers on that raft. They come up first."

Captain Riefkohl cursed and said, "No! Wounded men come first. We'll be last." So they took the crane and lowered a net down, and they laid me in the cargo net and another buddy of mine who had his chest blown out and barely breathing ... and they lifted us up.

They spread us survivors out on the deck all the way around the ship. That day the sun was very intense, and the deck was burning hot. I kept passing out and coming to and passing out because of loss of blood. The pain was so severe.

They had no morphine or any medicines to give us. It wasn't long before the guy next to me passed away.

After they had gotten all of the men out of the water that they could get, they steamed toward the hospital ship, USS SOLACE, anchored quite a ways out of the harbor. We were taken aboard, but there were so many of us, and they didn't have enough facilities, doctors and nurses to take care of all these casualties.

They took one look at me and told me that there wasn't much they could do for me. There wasn't enough morphine nor help. But they would take me along with a lot of the others and transfer me to a troop transport where they would try to operate, pull my leg out of my chest and cut it off. There were just too many casualties.

I don't know if these figures are correct but they say there were 1,200 men on the Vincennes and we lost all but about 200 because remember the torpedoes went into the fire room and the boiler room, and all of those men who were below deck didn't have a chance to get out.

An Australian cruiser lost all hands, and one of our light cruisers was beached and burned itself out on the shore. Another cruiser that was with us also had about the same casualty ratio that we had.

So the hospital ship took us to Wellington, New Zealand, where they transferred many of us to a mobile hospital. But they didn't have adequate surgical facilities to take care of us either. Finally, we were put aboard a troop transport. For me, it was one of the greatest miracles of my life.

I was on a gurney, and this doctor came in. He looked at me. I didn't have a dog tag ... I was so badly swollen. He said to me, "Who are you?" I gave him my name, rank and serial number. He said to me, "You look very familiar. I'm going to take you up to the makeshift operating room where we are going to take your leg off. Then we are going to see if we can straighten your back and your spine and put you in a cast up to your neck so we can get you home."

As I was lying on the operating table, he looked at me again and he said, "I should know you. I believe I do. You say your name is?" I gave him my name again, and he said, "I believe I brought you into this world. I'm your mother's doctor. I worked at the New Haven Hospital." Of course, New Haven, Connecticut, was my home town.

I imagine many questions were coursing through that doctor's mind: "Bill Lentsch, How on earth did you end up here?" "What on earth am I going to do with you now?" And probably, "What does the future hold for a mangled mess like you?"

HOPE FOR WOUNDED WARRIORS

CHAPTER 2: CONNECTICUT CHILDHOOD

The answer to that first question: "How on earth did you end up here?" is a combination of the dynamics of a dysfunctional family, some bad choices ... plus a good dose of divine providence. What the future held for a mangled mess like me, is the theme of the rest of this story. It has some dark pages ... some stuff I'm deeply ashamed of and embarrassed to talk about ... yet if this story would bring hope and inspiration to anyone, it has to include the dark stuff.

I was born William Edmund Lentsch on May 13, 1922, on Blachley Avenue, across the Quinnipiac River in New Haven, Connecticut. My parents were William and Genevieve Lentsch. It was in the depression days. My mother took in washing and ironing. My father worked in a hospital laundry.

It's a unique story how they met. My mother was 15. She had a very strict father. He would not allow her to date any boys; would not allow her to go near any boys ... so she ran away from home. The family was living in Daytona Beach, Florida. She hitchhiked to Atlanta, Georgia. Arriving with no money, she was tired and very hungry. She wandered into a hotel.

My father was 17, working on the desk as a night clerk in that hotel. Being very desperate, she asked him for help. He felt sorry for her, so he let her lounge in the lobby until five o'clock and saw that she had something to eat. In the morning he asked her where she was going. She didn't know. She had just run away from home.

So he said, "Why don't you just stay around here for awhile. I'll pay for your room. (In those days it was very low money.) I'll make sure you get something to eat, and we'll work out something." So she said, "Okay, it sounds fine to me." Remember now, this is in the early 1900's. So in exchange for cleaning rooms, she got her room and board.

They dated about 2 months. My dad said, "You know, you're a nice gal, why don't we get married?" She had just turned 16, and he turned 18, so they got a Justice of the Peace to marry them.

They continued there for a while, but she was afraid that her father, my grandfather, would find them. He was a disciplinarian, and he had the police looking for her, not realizing that they had gotten married. At the turn of the century you didn't need parental consent to get married.

So my father took his old model T Ford, packed all the stuff in it, and they drove to Gilford, Connecticut, where his father had a farm. But he soon grew tired of farm work and decided to seek work in the city where he got a job as a journeyman washer man in the laundry at a hospital in New Haven.

He worked himself up to being an overseer, sort of a supervisor. The next year my brother, Alvah, was born to them. Alvah was a lazy person with no desire to do anything but to run with a gang of delinquent boys. Their spending money came from selling parts stolen from cars.

Next door to the laundry on Blachley Avenue, there was a house that Dad rented for many years. Four years later I was born. I was named William Edmund Lentsch. I asked my mother one time who Edmund was. She said that it was the name of an old boyfriend of hers when she was in school. I asked, "Why did you name me after him?" She said, "To spite your dad--I didn't want you to be a junior." And so it was, I was named, Edmund.

My mother wanted a girl when I was born, so she dressed me as a girl until I went to school. I had long curly hair all the way to my shoulders, and I wore dresses. She called me "Billie" which is a girl's spelling, not the "Billy" which is a nickname for William. Of course, until I started to school, I didn't know the difference.

When I entered grade school the principal sent me home because I was a boy dressed in girl's clothes and had long curly hair. He sent a note home that they would not permit me in school until she dressed me as a boy, and enrolled me as a boy. She had enrolled me as a girl.

My mother was very unhappy--she wanted a girl so bad but complied with the school's wishes. She cut my hair-- put a bowl on my head and cut it around, and cut it in back. After elementary school I went to a commercial high school across the river for three years but didn't graduate.

My brother and I were not very close; he was 4 years older than me ... and he was a troublemaker. He spent more time in the Principal's office than in the classroom. So when I came to the same school, I had a difficult time overcoming his reputation.

But we did have some good times together. We used to take a boat and go out on the river. We'd go fishing, and also we would go crabbing. We would take a piece of raw meat, put it on a hook and drop it down a bank. The crabs that lived in the bank would come out and grab the meat which had a hook on it. We had lots of soft shelled crabs. At our house we went crabbing quite regularly in the summer months.

When winter came the river froze over. The ice was at least 4 to 6 inches thick. Instead of going across the bridge we would slide ourselves across the river to go to school and slide ourselves back.

The city allowed ice skating on the lake at the municipal golf course, so we played a lot of hockey and had a great time. We also did a lot of tobogganing on a hill which had about a quarter of a mile descent. Of course, back in the early 30's cars weren't too plentiful, so we almost had a clean street when it would snow. We had some good times sledding.

One year I was walking uphill ... pulling my sled behind me. I didn't get out of the way of one of the oncoming sleds. It hit me in the leg, cutting it all the way to the bone. In those days they didn't take you to the hospital. They took you home and tried to get a call into the doctor. That dedicated doctor came with his horse and buggy to the house and made a house call. I was laid up for a long time. They couldn't afford crutches or a cane.

That was about the only bad thing I had happen to me until later on when I came down a steep hill on my bicycle. At the bottom, the front wheel got caught in the trolley tracks. The bicycle flipped and catapulted me through the air. While no bones were broken and the scrapes and cuts healed quickly, the injury to the lower groin took six months for recuperation during which time my mother home-schooled me.

One day my friends and I were playing "Cowboys and Indians." They tied me to a pole and left me there. It was almost dark when my parents found me.

One winter we saw the snow drifted up to the second story window after a 3 day blizzard., My father would jump out the window and slide down to the door with a shovel and shovel a path to get out to the road.

With deep snow, when the snow plow came, it piled up real high and you couldn't get around. You had to cut a path into the street ... and there was nothing running except the snow plow. The trolleys could not run because the tracks were covered with ice and snow. We had to walk to the nearest store, hoping that they had some milk or bread left over from before the storm.

My sister Rose was born 9 years after I was. Mother finally got a girl and she was ecstatic. Being the fact that she took in washing and ironing, I fell to being her babysitter. I was 9 years old, and it was my job to diaper her and make sure that she got her bottle.

I remember many days playing piggyback with her on the floor. We just had a great time. Although I teased her a lot, she has fond memories of her childhood because we were so close.

We were always very poor, but there was a couple in the church who owned a farm way out from town, and they always felt sorry for us. My father made five dollars a week at the laundry but these are back in the depression days, and my mother didn't make much more than that.

We'd go out and pick dandelions in the spring of the year when they were tender and make dandelion soup. She'd take a little flour and mix it with dandelions or mustard

25

greens. People today probably would not eat dandelions, but if cooked with a chunk of salt pork, they are really good. Mother always baked bread to go with them to make a meal.

I remember the city ran a pig farm in conjunction with the collection of garbage. Some restaurant employees would be careless when they scraped the plates into the garbage. We would go to the pig pens and look for silverware. We found many knives, forks and spoons.

One Thanksgiving things were so tough that we only had bread and water ... but the church dropped off a large basket of food and a turkey. That was a very emotional time to have a real Thanksgiving dinner.

One Easter I asked my mother if I could go and visit my friend on a farm for Easter dinner. I knew they were going to have ham and that would be a treat as we could never afford ham. We didn't have much to eat ... only what they gave us off the farm to supplement what we could buy. So she said, "Yes, you can go visit your friend."

They picked me up at church in their Model A Ford and took me out to our house to get some things. Mother had saved (I don't know how much money) to buy me a coat and a pair of brand new shoes. She sacrificed for me to have those things for Easter. Normally I had "hand-me-downs" patches on patches from my brother's clothes.

When I left, my mother said, "There are two things that I am requiring of you. Don't go near the water. (There was a large stream that emptied into a nearby river.) And do not start a fire with matches out there. Everything is tinder dry, especially the trees at this time of the year with leaves on the ground. It might just set fire to the fields and barns. Will you promise me you won't do this?"

Keeping that in mind, I joyfully went off with my friend's family. I was about 10 years old. My sister was at home; she was the baby. It was a beautiful dinner. I remember we had turkey, vegetables, and ham. My friend says to me, "Let's go down to the river. It's swollen this time of the year because the snow is melting, and we'll watch the branches and the leaves going downstream."

It was a shallow river ... not too wide ...with a small island in the center. My friend said, "Let's play pirates. We'll take off our shoes and socks and wade over to the island. It's only two feet deep." Even though it was bitter cold, we still did it.

I decided to throw my shoes over to the island. Imagine the terror in my heart as I saw one fall short and be carried away by the current. Terrified at the thought of losing my shoe, I plunged after it but the water was swift and it was soon gone. I failed in my attempt to rescue my new shoe, but I succeeded in falling ... and getting soaking wet.

So my buddy says, "I'll gather up a lot of dry leaves, and we'll build a fire, and we'll dry you out". Oh! What a mistake! The wind was blowing and we did not build a rock place to hold the fire. Well, as you can imagine, the wind picked up, spreading the embers, and we soon had a forest fire going. Many of the pine trees, the Christmas tree type, were burning. It was roaring.

The fire department came ... which was most ancient. It was volunteers. They had to get people from town to come to surround this fire and control it. They kept the barn from catching fire, and eventually it burned itself out but my new coat was covered with pine tar as I had used it to try to beat out the flames of the fire.

When we got back to my friend's house, I told his mother that I had lost a shoe. When she took me home, she loaned me a pair of her shoes. My parents were going on to church that night. I was to go upstairs and get ready for bed because there was school the next day.

I decided that I could not hide the coat, but what do I do about the right shoe? Well, I decided to throw it in the closet under a bunch of newspapers and stuff, and then tell her that I couldn't find both of my shoes. Boy, did I put on a good act! In those depression days you didn't have 2 pairs of shoes.

When I got up in the morning, pretending to look for that shoe, I threw everything out of the closet. I had lost it, I couldn't find it anywhere. Well, I had told her about the coat, and she said that she forgave me. "But you had better not be lying about that shoe. If you are I'll whale the tar out of you to within an inch of your life." So I said, "Oh, no, Mom, I wouldn't lie to you". I missed 3 days of school while they scraped up enough money together to buy me another pair of shoes.

It had been dark the night before when I was wearing the lady's shoes home. I had hidden the other shoe under my coat. My mother didn't notice it because they got right in the car as I got out. That next Sunday at church she comes up to my mother and says, "Have you got my shoes?" My mother says, "What do you mean?" She says, "I lent them to Bill when he lost his shoe down the river."

I had not realized that I had to return the shoes. When we came home from church my mother was very angry. You could tell her face was getting red, she was so angry. Perhaps angry is really not the word to use. She was incensed!

Not only did I lie ... but to live a lie was more than she could stand!!!

We were all sitting around the table. After grace was said, she says to me, "William! William Edmund!" (She would call me that when she was angry.) "Do you want it now, or do you want it later? If you have it now, you are not going to sit down for a week. If you wait until later, your food will digest. You'll be better off if I do it later. Dad, I'll want the strap." (They had a black razor strap which they used against our legs when we were disobedient.) "Dad, go get the black strap. William is going to be punished."

So she took me by the ear and up the stairs. We went to my bedroom in the attic which I shared with my brother. She took my pants down to the bare behind, and she laid that strap on my bare behind a dozen times, and she raised welts.

She said, "You won't be able to rest, you won't sleep tonight. In the morning I'll put salve on the welts if you want it. But don't you tell anyone at school, I don't want anyone to know this. I'm embarrassed to death that you wore a lady's shoe and didn't tell me. How you could disobey me, I'll never understand." It was very difficult to sit in a classroom on a behind filled with welts. When she laid that strap on me she said, "That will teach you not to lie to your mother or anyone else."

When I was 12 years old I went to work in the YMCA setting pins in a bowling alley. I did that for 2 years and bought my own bicycle to ride over to the YMCA. I made more money than my father. He was making five dollars a week at the laundry. I was making 10 to 12 dollars a week setting pins in a bowling alley.

I worked until 11 o'clock at night and was up early the next day for school. I earned my money and turned it all over to the family except for a couple of dollars a week for school lunches and what have you. It helped them out but I sure got tired of peanut butter and jelly sandwiches every day and an apple.

Everything went along smoothly until my parents joined the Assembly of God church. I was saved in a great church meeting at age 8. I was baptized in April, 1930. There was snow on the ground. There was a brook that ran through a friend's farm, and they had hollowed it out for swimming. I was baptized in that water. It was ice cold and I nearly died when I went under. I came out and they wrapped towels around me. The air temperature must have been between 35 and 40 degrees, but I never developed a cold or became sick.

My mother and father were very devout Christians ... to a point. I'll tell you why I say "to a point". They had high principles, but their actions were often very carnal. Many times their arguments and their fights were of my father's doing. Father was insanely jealous. He repeatedly accused her of seeing another man, (which was true but she would never admit it at the time.)

One time my father picked up a butcher knife and was almost on my mother's neck when my 5 year old sister grabbed his hand. I was about 12 at the time and I jumped into the fray ... grabbing the knife out of his hand. When I did it, the knife sliced across her hand. They had to rush her to the hospital and she had 7 or 8 stitches. She carried the scar to her grave. She remembered the butcher knife incident very well. Our father was an extremely jealous man with a violent temper and constantly making accusations which mother denied. We all feared him.

Somewhere along in there my mother had met a man at church who was having trouble with his wife, and naturally she was having trouble at home and that's a drawing card. They were soon seeing each other regularly. I remember he was a big guy. He would always buy us ice cream when we would go. She would never go without her kids.

She would bring my sister and me along so that if anyone said anything was happening, it didn't happen because the two kids were along. His name was Al. My brother's name was also Al. He was a nice man and always treated us very fairly, though my sister says he tried to molest her after mother and he were married.

Finally, things came to a head and my folks divorced. Al also divorced his wife and they married. Meanwhile other things happened that were impacting my life.

I had just turned 14 when Russ Morgan's Band was in town auditioning for singers. I won the contest, and he invited me to go on tour with the Band. My mother said I was too young so instead I received a box of chocolate covered cherries ... quite a disappointment.

I remember my first encounter with a pipe. My father never allowed me to have any privileges. I wanted to smoke. So at 14 I would go behind the barn, get a bunch of dried cornsilk and put it in an old pipe and smoke it. I remember one Sunday when I had done that and became green around the gills, I was so sick.

My father came in and asked, "What's wrong with you? You look terrible. Do you think I should take you to a doctor?" I said, "No." He said, "Let me smell your breath." He could smell the smoke and realized what I had been doing. I said, "Dad, it was corn silk. It wasn't tobacco." He said, "I've

31

warned you not to smoke." He didn't punish me. I think he thought being sick was enough punishment for smoking corn silk.

That same year the divorce papers were filed. In a little town like New Haven, where Yale University is, it hit the papers. I remember the headlines ... some cruel thing like "Man attempts to kill wife; She divorces him for another man at church" or something like that. He had threatened her with a butcher knife. It was a sticky mess. I was so embarrassed. I wanted out of there!

CHAPTER 3: GEORGIA & THE FARM

One night, I slipped out of the house, went down to the highway and hit the road with my thumb. I was going to Florida to live with an uncle. He did not know I was coming. I had many kind people who took me on my way ... buying me a lunch etc. I hitch-hiked all the way down to Atlanta, Georgia, where it was raining so hard that it was throwing silver minnows off the gulf on to the highway.

I stood there soaking wet at the bus station and wondered, "How am I going to get to my destination from here?" I thank the Lord that a man came up to me and asked where I was going. He gave me enough bus fare to get to Daytona Beach where my mother's brother lived. He was an undertaker.

I remember the night I walked in and I said to him, "Uncle Charlie, Mother and Dad are divorced." He didn't know anything about it, so I explained to him what happened. "Well, you can stay here until I can find another place for you. I don't want you here permanently. Viola, my daughter, is 14 also, and I don't think it's healthy that 2 cousins are together."

He knew nature, and he explained it to me. I said, "I don't think you have anything to worry about." And he said, "Too many ... at that age. So I want you out of here." I said, "Okay."

He continued out loud, "I think I am going to get hold of Uncle Glen up at Valdosta, Georgia. He's got a farm up there, and see if you can stay there, because your grandmother is staying with him. (That's my mother's mother.) You could be a big help to him while you're there." So I said, "Well, that's fine with me", not realizing that I was going into slavery for the next 4 years as I had no idea what the conditions were. So he gave me bus fare to Valdosta, Georgia.

As I remember it, Valdosta, in the early 30's, was a rural, dusty one-building town. Within that one building was the post office, the dry goods store, grocery store, and the bus station. Outside were 2 gasoline pumps that you operated by hand because they had no electricity. That was Valdosta, Georgia ... a typical country town in the South.

My Uncle Glen had received 160 acres from the government to homestead. To get clear title he had 5 years to improve the land, build a house and barn. He had no help other than the African Americans, called "darkies", who would come to help him in the fall of the year to slaughter the hogs.

They would take the chitlins, the innards, and the hog's head for pay in return for slaughtering the hog. They would hang the hams, sides of bacon, and pork chops in the smokehouse to cure and then render the fat into lard for cooking.

I had never been exposed to that type of living. They had a three bedroom house that had aluminum siding all the way around, and the roof was aluminum too. When it rained, it made a sound like bombs were hitting the top of the roof because there was no insulation. We had coal oil lamps to read by, no electricity, and an outside privy, of course.

The nearest schoolhouse had 12 grades in one school 5 miles away, and nothing there except 2 ruts in the road which were made by wagons when it rained.

We had to walk the 5 miles in the morning and walk home in the afternoon. All he gave me were a pair of shoes, underwear and a pair of bib overalls--that's all he gave me. In return I became his personal slave. The shoes were to wear on Sunday ... all other days we went barefoot.

I'd get up in the morning at 4:30 and split the firewood for the stove which was the main item to cook on. My grandmother would get up at 4:30 or 5:00. I would split pine logs, which were full of turpentine, into long strips of wood. When you put them in the stove, drop a match in it, immediately there was instant fire. Then she would cook breakfast.

Ninety percent of the time breakfast on the farm constituted fried chicken, ribs, and toast made from homemade bread ... sometimes fried grits and bacon. Grandmother kept busy making jelly and canning chickens. Most of the eggs were used in her baking, not fried for breakfast.

So we'd get up in the morning, wash and clean up in a bucket of cold water pumped from the well, slop the hogs, get all the chores done and then I would be off to school. I was the only so-called "hired hand" ... the only boy to do all the chores. I'd come home from school and head for the fields. I would have to hack out all the weeds among the corn, and hack out all the weeds among the peanuts.

My uncle grew a lot of peanuts which he fed to the hogs to fatten them up. There were also sweet potatoes to weed ... which is why I hate to eat sweet potatoes. That was the main meal for us in the evening ... sweet potatoes and left over cold chicken. Baths were taken in a large kettle also used for watering the cattle. Grandmother would heat water on the wood stove for our Saturday night baths.

One night we heard a terrible squealing down in the hog pen which was 800 or 900 feet from the Swanee River.

There were alligators which lived in the Swanee River and at night they roamed the banks looking for food. Some of the alligators were 8 feet long and almost 2 feet across at the front shoulders.

My uncle grabbed the shotgun, and I went with him in the old pickup truck down to the hog pen. There was this huge alligator with a hog's hind leg in his mouth ... trying to swallow it. So my uncle took aim with the shotgun and wham, he hit that alligator, killed it, threw it back into the water and left. The next day we had to slaughter the hog as it was too badly injured to live.

The colored neighbor came over, prepared a huge black pot of boiling water and dipped the hog in it to scrape off all the hair. Then we started cutting it up. We took the hams, bacon and all these things and put them in the smokehouse. The neighbor got the chitlins, sowbelly, etc. for helping us.

There was another time when we were walking along the Swanee River. My uncle wore big boots up to above his knees and he loaned me a pair of his boots. He said that the reason for the boots was that the rattlers down here were bad and I don't want you to get bit because we have no doctor within miles of this place.

We were walking and he yells, "Stop!" I remember stopping and I froze in my tracks. Just as he raised up his shotgun, I saw this big rattlesnake--huge thing as long as this room -- ready to strike. His rattler was going like mad, and my uncle blew off its head.

It lay there, and I went over and asked if I could pick it up and make a belt or something out of it. He said not to touch it until the sun goes down. Those things can still bite you, they are still alive. So we let it lay there overnight.

The next day he went and picked it up and skinned it. This is why you don't come down into this swampy area without high boots on. If it strikes you above your boots you are dead. There was no anti-venom available to help you, and the nearest hospital was in Atlanta 160 miles away.

My grandmother was in her 80's and had loved me as a mother loves a child. She was a grand old lady and lived to be 96. Meanwhile I attended the one room school house for 3 different grades.

When I turned 17 I said to myself that it was time for a change. I said, "Uncle Glen, I have worked for you for 3 years." He said, "What do you want to do?" I told him that I wanted to join the Navy. He asked if I was tired of being a farmer. I replied that I wanted to get away and do something different.

He wanted to know what I wanted from him. I wanted a suit, tie, shirt, shoes, socks, and some underwear. He agreed that I had earned it, so he took me into town to the store and bought me the new clothes. Then he took me by mule up to the railroad station, bought me a ticket and put me on the train for home.

HOPE FOR WOUNDED WARRIORS

CHAPTER 4: U.S. MARINE CORPS – BASIC TRAINING

Upon arrival back in Connecticut, I took a bus to the old house where we used to live. My father was still living there. He told me where my mother and her husband, Al, were living.

I had known Al from the 5 years they had been secretly meeting. He had divorced his wife and married my mother. Together they had purchased a five acre chicken ranch up near Gilford and had a comfortable home. Al had an egg route and sold eggs, butter and chickens.

I told my mother that I wanted to join the Navy but she didn't want me to. I was only 17 and she thought I didn't know what I wanted. I said, "I'm not going to live here with this man, he's not my father." She said that Rose is going to be here. She was about 8 years old. My brother had left home at age 18 and joined a gang of car thieves about the time I had gone to Georgia.

I did not want to stay there, I resented Al. Maybe in a way I thought that it was his fault. Both my father and mother had been very religious people in a carnal sense. They knew about Jesus but they did not know him in a personal way. On Sundays I couldn't read the funny papers; if I read anything it had to be the Bible or other religious material.

So I told my mother that in all fairness to me "you'll sign some papers and let me go down and enlist." She said, "I really don't want you to do that." I said, "Mom, the war is coming. They are drafting. I registered for the draft and when I turn 18 I'll have to go into the Army. And I don't want to go into the Army. I want to go into the Navy or something like the Navy. I want to be out on the water."

She looked at Al and said, "What do you think?" He responded, "I think he's old enough to make his own decision. If you want to let him go, I would suggest you sign the papers, because he's only going to mope around here for a year. Then he'll go do it anyway." She said, "I don't think they'll take you."

I had a serious injury when I was 13 which laid me up for over 8 months. I said, "I have enough money left over from my trip home, and I'm going to take a train down to New York City to go to a recruiting office. I'll be home probably this afternoon." Little did she know that I would not come back until after my basic training.

I took the train and went to the Navy recruiting office, walked in and said, "I want to join the Navy." I went down to the Navy doctor and stripped down to my skivvies. He measured my chest. I only weighed 125 lbs. and was a skinny kid. He said, "I'm sorry. The Navy can't use you. Why don't you go through that doorway. There's another service next door which might suit you to a T."

I was a dumb 17 year old kid. I went through the door, and the doctor was right behind me. He brought all my clothes over there. He says, "Oh, hi! Let's measure your chest with a Marine tape. Just right! Put up your right hand." The recruiter came in to swear me in to the Marine Corp. I asked if I might get into the Navy if I became a Marine. He said, "Oh, you might go to sea school and become a sea going Marine."

So he swore me in to the Marine Corp and said they were sending me down to the Hotel Astor to stay until the following morning. The rest of the Marines will meet you there and you'll go down to the train and on to Perris Island, South Carolina.

Getting back to my brother ... he was in a gang of car thieves. In those days they used to remove fenders, wheels, tires, windshield wipers. Even take convertible tops off. They had a place where they would store all this stuff.

On Saturday they would have a sale. If people needed parts for cars, they would buy them. He was into this way up to his ears. He was making all kinds of money. He was just really enjoying himself. He wasn't worried about the draft. He was 4 years older than I. They did call him, and the irony is he also enlisted in the Marines.

My father eventually met another lady and he remarried. They moved up to near Stamford, Connecticut. He went to work as a laundry foreman up there. She was a very, very, very hard lady. She was hardened on a farm in Kansas, very weather-beaten type, very bossy. She bossed my dad around quite a bit. He didn't seem to mind, he was content to have a helpmate.

I never had much to do with him after that. She kind of sheltered him from us kids. He passed away when he was 80 ... had a massive stroke. He was working in a parking garage giving out tickets,, and he went home one night and died. My stepmother called to tell me. She said he was going up to bed, and when he reached the top of the stairs, she heard a thump when he hit the floor. She ran up and he was gone. My mother died about 10 years after he did from a brain tumor.

In July, 1939, I went to Perris Island. We had about 30 men with us. They issued me 2 sets of khakis and showed me my bunk. We were to begin training the next morning.

That night a bunch of old salts came into the barracks to shoot dice and to play poker. I'll never forget it. They invited me to join with them. I still had a little money in my pocket. These old salts knew they could clean out these new recruits before payday. We received $30 a month.

I saw this sergeant slip an ace up his sleeve. Of course, innocent me, not realizing that these guys are tough, I called him. "I saw you slip an ace up your sleeve." He got mad. He said, "Don't you tell me that I'm cheating. I'm a sergeant. I don't have to show you anything. If you insist, I am going to teach you a lesson so that you'll never forget"

With that he picked me up by the collar, and wham, he hit me with his fist, and I ended up against the wall. Bruised and battered I went to my bunk. The next morning I was sore. It taught me a lesson -- you don't do that. I learned other lessons in boot camp too.

It was a hot July, and they were drilling us on the cadence. Guys were dropping like flies, even the corporal was soaking wet. They drilled us all the way down to the beach and into the water with our rifles over our heads, then cadences back to the mess hall. We walked into the mess hall dripping wet, sat down, and put our rifles up against the benches.

The older groups were making fun of us and taunting us. You know, those drill sergeants were nasty and mean. One recruit failed to clean his rifle, and he called it a gun. They stripped him naked and made him stand holding the bar on the window of the paymaster's office with one hand and the rifle in the other hand for half an hour, saying, "This is not a gun. This is my rifle." I thought, "I got to keep straight. I don't want that to happen to me."

We had to clean our rifles every night, and they inspected them the next day. We spent 2 weeks drilling, getting in shape. The third week a hurricane hit the island and we were all herded into old brick barracks. Everything on base was destroyed except the brick buildings. I have the pictures today.

The next day when the storm had subsided there were yachts and every conceivable boat beached on the island, seaweed up to your knees. We spent 2 weeks cleaning that island which extended our time there longer than for the normal recruit.

We went out to the rifle range one day to qualify as marksmen/sharp shooters. When those "03" rifles recoil they hit you in the shoulder. They will knock you flat and loosen your teeth if you don't know how to hold them. I had a bruised shoulder where that rifle hit me time and again.

The strange thing was we learned how to use it ... including bayonet practice. It never occurred to me that I was training to go into the trenches to fight the enemy with a bayonet.

One night the sergeant and the lieutenant notified the platoon that they were going to town in Charleston, South Carolina, and we'd be on our own. You don't want to do that with a bunch of raw recruits. Little did we realize it was a test!

After we saw the jeep go down the road one of the guys said, "Let's get up a game of poker." In those days you didn't do that in boot camp. You didn't gamble, you didn't play cards. I said, "I'll be the lookout. When I see the jeep coming down the roadway I'll holler."

Something happened. They came back without their lights on, and we didn't know that. They expected us to be up to something ... and they walked in on this poker game. It made the corporal so mad. He ordered the guys to strip off all their clothes, get their rifles and go out and drill.

The mosquitoes were so thick that you could cut them with a knife. Here we were stark naked, marching down into the swamp. He had mosquito netting over his hat and clothes covering him. He drilled us for an hour in the mud and reeds of the swamp near the ocean. I had a cut across my foot from stepping on the reeds.

The next morning when we got up for inspection, we looked like we had the measles. We were covered with red splotches all over our faces, arms and legs, and all swollen up. The lieutenant who was in charge demanded, "What went on last night?"

Mum's the word. "I want an answer. Something went on here last night because of the shape you are in. You can't even drill anymore because your feet are all cut up. I want someone to tell me."

He had us in the squat position for an hour with our rifle over our head but no one would speak up. It was hot and humid, we were miserable, and our feet hurt. He said, "Somebody is up for a court-martial. There are only 2 men who could have done this, the sergeant or the corporal. I was out with the corporal so it couldn't be him. It has to be the sergeant."

Little did he know that it happened after they got back, and it was the corporal who did it. This corporal had spent 20 years in China on duty with the Marine Detachment. He had no compassion for others. He was as mean as a rattlesnake and his bite was just as bad.

So they were going to put the sergeant up and court-martial him. I couldn't stand that. I was so upset because it was so unfair. He had nothing to do with it. He had gone on liberty as well. So after we could relax I went up and knocked on the door of the lieutenant. I said, "Sir, the corporal did it." He asked, "How do you know?"

I said, "Look at me. I'm so bitten with mosquito bites and my feet are cut. I was in that group; I know. I know he'll kill me ... This is cruel." Little did he know about the other stuff that went on. No one had ever told him. Everyone feared him. Remember he had control over the platoon and whatever he said was law.

He said, "You did the right thing. You'll have to testify at the trial." I said, "Sir, I don't want to be there. I don't want any part of this. I'm just telling you the truth so you don't accuse a man falsely." He said, "All right, you won't have to testify. But if push comes to shove I may need you. I may need to put you on the stand. I don't want to if we can get away without it." I was afraid for the repercussions when the corporal got freed.

They held a court-martial for the corporal. He was accused of brutality. The general wanted to know who told. So I testified and asked to be permitted to tell my side of the story. "The corporal had been in town, and he was pretty drunk when he came back to base. That isn't a good excuse for what he did, but we were gambling. We were partially at fault. And I think in fairness to him you need to take this into consideration."

45

The general looked at me and said, "You make a lot of sense. We'll consider that in our deliberations. You are excused." The corporal ... they stripped him to Pfc. and they shipped him out to other duty, but he did me a lot of damage. Before he left he put in my folder that I was a poor Marine and a disgrace to the service, and that he would not recommend me for anything.

I was up for sea duty. I had volunteered to go to sea school because then you could go aboard a Navy vessel. I was a half inch short of the five foot eight requirement, but they had a quota and they needed me, so they told me I could go. I took the train up to Norfolk, Virginia.

After I got there, the Sergeant in charge called me into the office and said, "You have a terrible mark against you in your files by corporal so and so." I said, "We had some problems, and I was called into court to testify against him." He said, "I want to tell you this; I judge a man by his performance under my leadership, not under somebody else's. I don't care about the circumstances that got this in your file, but if you'll perform for me, and you learn from me as I teach you, and you graduate from sea school with a good grade, I'll take this out of your file." Praise the Lord for His guidance in this matter.

We had lots of fun at sea school. We got into all kinds of trouble as usual. We would go to school during the day, and take shifts at night guarding the ships in the Navy yard.

They would assign us to a ship to walk up and down in front of them. We had a 45 automatic. If we were to see anybody who did not have the proper papers, we immediately put a gun in their back and took them to headquarters. So that was our job.

I remember one night when it was about 20 degrees below zero. It was cold. Oh, it was freezing. The Navy ship brought in coffee from Brazil, and I could smell that coffee and wanted coffee so bad. There was a guard shack away from my post, and a civilian guarding the lumber yard. I could see that potbellied stove glowing red.

I decided to leave my post and get in that guard shack and get warm. So I did. I leaned back in the chair and fell asleep. I guess I slept for at least an hour. Near daybreak I could hear the motor on the approaching relief truck. I slipped out of the office and ran along behind it, and slipped on to my post.

The lieutenant comes up and says, "Where have you been?" I said, "Well, I tell you sir, I don't know what happened to the civilian guard, but I heard noises in the lower yard. It was off my post, I know, but I had to go and check them out." He said, "You are lying through your teeth. You were sitting in that guardhouse asleep." I said, "Sir, you can't prove that."

"No, I can't prove that, " he said, "but I believe it. Get in the truck." I got relieved. Every day after that if I saw him, I would cross the street. I did not want to get near this guy.

The day came when we graduated. Oh, happy day! The Sergeant gave me a good grade. I learned to take care of .45 caliber automatics, machine guns, Browning Automatic Rifles and several other weapons.

We had liberty that night before we were ready to ship out. We went into town. I can't say all the details of what we went in to. It was a red light district and we were involved with some of the girls over there. One of the "Ladies of the Evening" wanted to marry me. She was about my age.

I told her that when I came back, we could get married. This is my past, forgive me.

This is the story. I got drunk so bad that I was lying in the gutter and passed out. And I'm supposed to be shipped out the next day. My buddy was trying to dry me up on the sidewalk. Finally he got me sobered up enough to get on the trolley and go back to the base.

I had turned my rifle in that morning to have a new rifle bore put in it, and I had not notified the major that I had done this. They had a group designated to go to Panama to be part of the fleet there. I called the shop in the morning and they said it would not be ready for another day or two. So I had no rifle.

They won't ship you anywhere without your rifle. That rifle goes with you until the day you die. It is part of your body. You are right up against it all the time. You sleep with it, you eat with it. So I said, "What am I going to do? And he said, "You just don't make it with the group."

That was a bad mistake. The group in Panama saw no war or action and had liberty every night.

Dumb me, I didn't go to the Major and tell him. When he came up to inspect the barracks all the guys had gone, and I'm sitting on my bed playing my harmonica. He walked up to me and said, "What are you doing here?" Again, this time shouting, "What are you doing here?"

I said, "My rifle is in survey to be repaired, Sir. I couldn't leave without it." He said, "Who gave you permission to put it in survey?" I said, "Well, Sir, I didn't get permission. I just knew it had a bad bore, and I had to have a new bore put in."

The major said, "I had to have so many men in that group and now I am missing one." I said, "I'm sorry, Sir." He said, "I'm going to get you out of here if it is the last thing I do. I understand you lied to my lieutenant; you got drunk; you come down here with a black eye because you've been in a fight. You're trouble. I've got to get rid of you." So I said, "Well Sir, I'm sorry, Sir. What would you have me do?" He said, "You're shipping out of here as soon as I can get a place to send you."

The heavy cruiser USS Vincennes called asking for one Marine to come aboard in the Brooklyn Navy Yard ... to fill their count. The Major replied, "I have just the man for them. His name is Private First Class Lentsch. I'll ship him up there to New York on the first train out." The rifle was sent up to me before the Navy ship left, and I went aboard the Vincennes as part of the Marine complement.

HOPE FOR WOUNDED WARRIORS

CHAPTER 5: USS VINCENNES

The naval ship, the USS Vincennes, a heavy cruiser, was tied up at the dock at the Brooklyn Navy Yard. The train left me at the station in downtown New York. A Sailor was waiting there with a Navy truck to take me to the ship.

When we got to the ship they took me aboard and introduced me to the Captain. From there I was taken down to the Marine quarters where I stowed away my clothes in the locker. The locker was 2 x 2 feet. It was a real small locker but if you folded things properly the way they taught, you could get everything in there except your pants. You put them under the mattress.

I was taken top side to help the work crew after I had changed into work clothes. This huge crane was lifting skids of bags of rice, beans, flour, sugar and all those staples that a cook needs to do his job. Also, they were loading cases of apples, bananas, pears and anything else that was available for that time of year. We worked until dark, secured the area, and then went down to the mess hall.

The ship was laid out very nicely, I thought. Sick bay was on the forward side of our compartment, and the paymaster's office and the library were on the other side ... and then the mess hall. So it was convenient for us Marines.

We had a contingency of quite a few Marines aboard, and our basic job was to man the two 5 inch antiaircraft guns. We had an old gunnery sergeant who had many years in the corps. He was ready for retirement at any time. We spent most of the days training on the guns.

The Vincennes made a North Atlantic patrol with orders to pursue the German Pocket Battleship "VON TERPTES". It was said to be close to Iceland. For several days we cruised, looking and listening for that ship. There were many icebergs in the area. We sighted the German ship about 12 miles north and tried to get within shooting range. No doubt they spotted us, plus we were hindered in intercepting them by the icebergs.

That night a northeaster storm came and we were tossed about. With waves breaking over us, we rolled 50 degrees sideways. The rain, snow and ice froze on the decks inches thick. In order to eat we had to hold onto something with one hand and our tray of food with the other. The storm blew winds 50 miles an hour all night. When it cleared the next day we had lost sight of the German ship.

We returned to New York and then continued on down to Trinidad where we took on supplies and headed for South Africa. The log says we landed in Capetown, but for some reason I remember it being "Simons Town".

We picked up a shipment of gold bullion there. It was lend-lease gold. The Marines on board were in charge of guarding the gold. Because the gold bars were so soft, upon arrival in Norfolk where the gold was unloaded, the Marines were examined very carefully ... not only under their fingernails, but even their stools for two days ... to be sure no gold had been stolen.

En route to South Africa, we crossed the Equator. There is always an initiation for Sailors and Marines as they cross that line. So we had to go through the different things they had set up on the ship. There was a canvas chute filled with garbage that we had to climb through, and many other rituals.

We became "shellbacks" with a certificate showing we had been duly inaugurated into King Neptune's Society. It was quite an interesting ordeal to go through. I didn't enjoy it but I realized that all the Navy personnel on ships did it at that time.

[Editor's Note: According to the certificate in Bill's scrapbook this transpired on 20 November 1941 at 139-40 degrees W. Other details of the trip can be found in a book, A Log of the Vincennes by Lieut. (Jg) Donald Dorris.]

When we got underway, the tugs pulled us away from the docks at the Brooklyn Navy Yard and we headed south through the Caribbean islands, over to Panama, and thru the Panama Canal, and then up the west coast to the Mare Island Navy Yard.

As we pulled into San Francisco Bay, the tugs pulled us into a drydock. There they secured our ship and pumped the water out. It took two or three days for the metal to dry, but when the ship was dry they painted the camouflage on the ship.

It took a few days to dry also. During that length of time we took on fresh water, more stores including fruit, vegetables, and other staples that we needed, and, of course, the mail came.

As the week progressed the Captain came on the ship's loudspeaker and said that we were going on a secret mission. It was strictly a volunteer mission; and for those who wanted to go, if they had anything against them, brig time, anything that caused them to have demerits on their record ... everything would be erased.

They would be set free from the brig if they made this trip. Anybody who didn't want to go would be transferred to

53

another ship. As it was, no one wanted to transfer. So we headed north to the Aleutian Islands and then west toward Japan.

As we went, we had a rendezvous with an aircraft carrier that had a lot of B-25 bombers on the deck. We had a light cruiser with us, two destroyers, and this aircraft carrier.

As each day evolved, we realized we were getting closer and closer to Japan, though we hadn't had any information from our officers as to where we were going. It was becoming a little worrisome. When we were still some distance from Japan, our engines slowed down, and we looked over at the aircraft carrier USS Hornet.

All the B-25s were lined up, and we wondered how they could take off from such a short deck. We learned later that they were tied down with ropes. When they were at full throttle the ropes were released, and they could lift off the carrier deck without a long runway. When they were all in the sky, Jimmy Doolittle in the lead plane dipped his wings at us and headed for Japan.

Not too long after we had the radio on and could hear the explosions. The Japanese said we had bombed hospitals and schools and there were many casualties. That's the last we heard.

We turned around and headed back to Hawaii at full speed ... thirty-eight knots on our ship. It just shook so bad we thought it might fall apart, but we had to get out of the area.

We had spotted a light ship that we had blown out of the water, and also a reconnaissance plane that we had shot down out of the sky. We figured the Japanese, with what fleet they had, would be coming after us. We left a huge wake behind us. All the ships were side by side as we crossed the International Date Line.

Well, we made it back to Pearl Harbor safely and prepared for a new mission. There we took on ammunition, the shells we needed to do the jobs we were assigned to do. We also got some fresh milk and topped off the fresh water tanks.

That night we pulled out under the cover of darkness and headed south to the Coral Sea. There we were engaged in the battle with part of the Japanese Navy in that area, trying to secure the South Pacific for our future, and to protect our States and the Hawaiian Islands.

I recall one aircraft carrier that really looked very lopsided. It was a converted troop ship that they had cut off the top and put on a flight deck so that planes could land and take off. It really wasn't practical, but in those days we didn't have the proper equipment to do the jobs we do today. Today everything is computerized and mechanized so we don't need the manpower that was used in those days.

After we defeated the small task force of Japanese ships, we steamed back to Hawaii, took on stores and ammunition. We had heard that the Japanese were coming with their fleet down to attack Midway Island. Their air force had already gone in and was bombing the beaches. It was our responsibility to go. So we headed out.

When we got around the location of Midway Island, we encountered the Japanese. We didn't see any ships but there were a lot of planes. There were dive bombers, torpedo bombers, high altitude bombers, all coming at us ... dropping their bombs ... firing their torpedoes at us, and dive bombers coming down directly at us.

During the battle of Midway we shot down several Japanese planes. We did not receive even one torpedo hit, but we could see many of them as they went whizzing by us. The Captain maneuvered the ship left and right and around as the torpedo bombers were coming at us.

One of the dive bombers went down the stack of an aircraft carrier and set the ship afire. They put it out, of course, but it was pretty much disabled. Later on, after the battle was over, sea going tugs came and pulled it into port. It was a fierce battle.

We went back to Hawaii, and after we took on food and water and substantiated our positions, we headed south for the Solomon Islands. We had gotten word from the Admiral of Task Force 68 that we would be part of the battle group that would go down to Guadalcanal and help the Marines secure the island.

As we progressed south, we encountered a couple of troop ships with Marines and landing equipment headed for the Fiji Islands. Our government had made arrangements that on one of the sparse islands where there were not many natives, the people would be moved at government expense to the other side of the island.

They didn't take any of their livestock with them. They just took their belongings, and the government said they would take care of their housing and protect them from any problems.

The next morning at daybreak we shelled the island with our 5 inch antiaircraft shells. In a mock landing, the Marines landed with their landing craft and went ashore and set up a beachhead. I learned that this practice would take place for a couple of days, and we were prepared to continue that bombardment of the island.

Every night we could see little bonfires on the beach. We heard the Marines had taken the pigs that were penned up that the islanders had left, and they were having pork luaus. They were really enjoying themselves. These were the troops that would be landing in a day or two on Guadalcanal.

After the bombardment of the island stopped and the Marines had reloaded back on the ships, we made our way into the Solomon Islands and into the Guadalcanal harbor. The harbor had two entrances, one at the top of the island, the other at the bottom. If you went thru the bottom one you probably would eventually wind up in New Guinea, going toward Australia. The other one would lead you to Iwo Jima and the other islands in the chain.

The Japanese were very well entrenched at Guadalcanal. ... had been there for a while. They had dug many defensive positions, trenches as you would call them ... because Henderson Airfield was there where they could land their planes with supplies, take out the sick, and whatever they wanted to do. It was a good landing strip there.

Our object was to rout them so that we could take over Henderson Field. When we went to Pule, Iwo Jima and the other islands, we would need a supply line. The planes could come in, and we could use that as a base.

We did not know how many Japanese were on this island nor how many were entrenched in caves and fortifications. We had reconnaissance showing they had a full division living on the island. Our carrier planes had bombed and strafed the island for many days until we felt we had softened up the enemy.

I'll never forget the morning that we arrived in Guadalcanal harbor. It was at 04:00 hrs. in the morning, dark, and we were called to our gun positions. As we approached, we lined ourselves up parallel with the beaches.

Just as dawn was breaking at 05:00 hrs. we started shelling the island with star shells. These shells, when they are fired into the air, float down to the earth with a burning light which lights up the beaches and have a war head on them that blows up when they hit their target.

We Marines would shoot with our five inch gun, and then the ship would swing around, and the crew on the other side would shoot their gun. The ship would swing around and we would fire ours again.

This went on until 06:00 hrs. in the morning. By that time it was fully daylight. The landing craft dropped off the ships that were with us. We watched the Marines go in and set up shop on the island beaches.

There was stiff resistance even though we had bombarded the island quite heavily. Despite severe casualties among the Marines, they managed to get a foothold and eventually take Henderson Field and wait for the Army to come and relieve them so they could move on to other conquests. The Army, under General MacArthur's command, did not come until six weeks later.

It was a difficult time because we didn't know where the Japanese Navy was. We were told that the USS North Carolina and the USS Washington, both battleships, were on the other side of the island of Guadalcanal. We didn't know, at least the crew didn't know, that the Japanese were off Savo Island northwest of our position.

We continued circling around Guadalcanal Harbor. That next morning the Japanese fleet sent in planes to bomb our troops and to bomb the ships that were in the harbor. There were three cruisers in the harbor: the Vincennes, the Quincy and the Canberra (Australian cruiser), plus two light cruisers, the Astoria and the Nashville.

For three days they pounded us with high altitude bombers dropping thousand pound bombs toward us, and torpedo bombers coming in at ship level, and 50 caliber machine guns strafing us, and also kamikaze planes trying to crash into our ship.

We had a good Captain. Captain Riefkohl managed to keep the ship from being hit by doing a lot of maneuvering. Of course, we were firing the anti-aircraft guns and the bonbon guns on the fantail of the ship. The 16 inch guns were useless for this sort of thing.

That went on for three days. During that time we had no solid food. Basically, we just had water to drink, because all the cooks were manning guns and had no time to do any amount of cooking.

Finally at the end of the third day, things quieted down. The admirals told our Captain they would alert us as soon as the Japanese were spotted coming down the coast to attack us. It was always said that they would attack with the "Rising Sun".

Well, apparently there was some lack of communication. Before the sun rose that morning, the USS Vincennes would be at the bottom of the sea and my life ... and many others would be forever changed.

HOPE FOR WOUNDED WARRIORS

CHAPTER 6: RECOVERY & REHABILITATION

I owe a lot to that doctor. He brought me into this world ... and then, upon recognizing me on the make-shift operating table of that troop ship ... he made a very crucial choice.

After looking at my leg that was broken in 18 places ... and having pulled it out and laid it out straight, he said, "Well, I think maybe I can save it. I don't know, but there is a new apparatus that I have with me called a 'Strader Splint'."

Then he explained, "I'll have to drill two holes, one at the top of your leg and the other hole below the knee. Then we'll put in the bolts across those to bolt them down and then spread that break open. Then I'll cut it open right through to that point and wire up all the biggest pieces of bone together ... hopefully we can save your leg."

Then he paused, "But I have a problem. I can't operate until we get some morphine. We don't have anything to stop the pain." I said, "Doc, I can hardly stand the pain. I'm just passing out all the time, I'm in such pain. Just go ahead and operate. I'll pass out and when I come to it'll be over with."

So he gave me a tongue depressor and I bit down on it and he drilled the holes through, top and bottom, and put in the "Strader Splint". When I woke up I was in a plaster body cast up to my neck and down to my toes ... with just the necessary openings.

The next day we were transferred to the mobile hospital in Auckland, New Zealand. They didn't have any morphine either. All they were doing was giving shots of sterile water, making believe they were morphine, and psychologically it worked. Once you got the shot, in a few minutes you would go off to sleep.

Three nights later I was told by an orderly not to say a word. When darkness fell, the orderlies came in with stretchers, and those men that they thought could be moveable and make it back to the States were taken down to the dock and loaded aboard a converted luxury liner.

They put me in a cabin right next to a porthole which was nice. Remember now, I was in a plaster cast from the top of my head to the tip of my toes. It was nice because I could look out the window of the porthole and see what was going on out at sea.

We weren't out of New Zealand more than a day or two ... it was at night, and the ship's engines stopped. We weren't moving. One of the orderlies came through and said, "Quiet, there's a Japanese convoy on the horizon. We have no lights and no engines going, so if there are submarines, they can't spot us or hear us and blow us out of the water." Even though we had a big red cross painted on the side of the ship, it still didn't mean anything to the enemy.

So I looked out the porthole, and they were going across on my side. I could see them quite clearly. All the ships had lights on them and that's so silly. You would think they would be dark, but they weren't. They had lights on, and you could see them going across the horizon. They felt very secure because they thought they had the Pacific pretty much wrapped up as to their area.

Because our fleet was inferior, they didn't have to worry about being attacked. If they did, they felt they could take care of us. Of course most of their crews were sleeping except those who were operating the ships. You couldn't tell what was in the convoy, but it was about an hour long. Finally, when the last light disappeared and it was gone over the horizon, our engines were started and our lights went on and we headed eastward toward home.

We came in somewhere down below Nicaragua. You could see all the lights along the shore line. We were not too far out ... just out deep enough to not run aground. We moseyed up the coast, and in a day or two approached San Diego. About three miles out from San Diego we encountered an enemy submarine. Fortunately they respected the huge Red Cross on our ship and did not attack us.

When we arrived in San Diego, at the Balboa Naval Hospital they did not know we were coming because of radio silence. We didn't want the Japanese to be able to pick up the signals coming from the ship or the hospital so it came as a total surprise to them.

They cleared out all the ambulatory patients and even the nurses' quarters. At that time some were staying off base. They had little places they were using while they were on duty. They were emptied out, and they brought in all the survivors on stretchers.

I remember the Vice Admiral who was in charge of the hospital greeted each one of us with a smile. He had a quart of whiskey in one hand and little cups on the table. We would be brought up and stopped ... and he would give each of us one of these and said, "This is for medicinal purposes. You must drink it. It is an order from the doctor."

You could almost choke, it was so bad. But we had orders to drink what little there was. It wasn't much ... sort of just a little jigger of it. But it was enough. I guess he had a reason for it. Each man or each person who came through the line who was wounded had to have a drink.

So we were taken in, and I was laid in a bed. The next day they took me to surgery. They cut the cast off me. The cast had been on now for about four weeks. They cut it off and put a leg cast on up to the hip and put me in traction in the bed. They took the "Straiter splint" off and inserted the bed traction devices. I was in the bed traction for about six weeks.

I remember the movie stars came to visit. Joan Blondel stopped by the bed and patted my hand and told me how proud she was of the troops that were wounded for their country, and all this blah blah blah business. But anyway, a lot of the comedians came through and different entertainers. They did a good job, really, when you consider the circumstances in the war.

The day that Joan Blondel visited, they had a photographer along from LIFE magazine. He took our pictures. In the issue of LIFE magazine for November 16, 1942, they published my picture on page 43 with the words, "Private W. E. Lentsch, 20, of New Haven, Conn. was caught in compartment of sunk Vincennes."

I had another major operation where they took the cast off the leg. Gangrene had set in, and they had to clean the wound out. They didn't sew it up. They just put maggots there to eat the gangrene away and covered it with Vaseline gauze. I was there about six months.

I couldn't walk without crutches. I couldn't put any weight on that leg at all. It hurt so bad. My spine hurt and so one day the doctor came by and he says, "How you doing there, fellow?" I said, "Well, I guess I'm doing ok. You guys know more about it than I do." And he said, "Well, don't worry about it. We're going to fix you up and get you back in battle." Well, I could have raised up and socked him one, but I smiled and he smiled back and walked away.

About two weeks later the head of the hospital came down and asked, "How would you like to be transferred to the Brooklyn Naval Hospital? We need this space for incoming wounded off of Guadalcanal, Iwo Jima, and these other islands.

We're having a lot of casualties coming in and they have space available there in Brooklyn. Your home is in Connecticut, so if you would like to transfer, I think we can arrange for a couple of Waves to go with you. Waves, of course, were girl sailors and nurses. So I said, "Fine. I would be glad to go."

So with me on crutches and a plaster cast on my leg, the two of them helped me aboard a train and took care of all of my needs. We rumbled for three or four days across the country into Chicago, and from there on into New York City to Grand Central Station ... the same station that I had left many months before to go aboard the heavy cruiser, USS Vincennes. Now I returned as a war casualty. Thankfully, my arm had healed up pretty good. They had taken a few stitches in it and I was able to get by pretty good. It wasn't really any problem.

They took me to Brooklyn Naval Hospital, and there they put me in a bed on the second floor near a window where I could look out and see the surrounding area. I don't know. I didn't feel as comfortable at the Brooklyn Naval as I did in San Diego Balboa.

Somehow or other I felt like they didn't really know the war. They hadn't yet felt the effects of the war. They hadn't been around any of the wounded. And I don't know, I just felt like those in San Diego had a better touch with what was going on out in the South Pacific. But that's my personal opinion.

As soon as I was brought in with my records, the doctor took the Vaseline gauze off and the cast and cleaned out the wound. He said that it was looking good but it still had a terrible drain, and it looked like I had osteomyelitis (That's probably not the word but I had an infection in there.)

They were trying their best at that time to stop the infection, but were not having too much success. I was in a wheelchair, so now I could be wheeled around the hospital and outside on the grounds. That did give me some more privileges. But they really didn't do as good as I thought they could have done.

One night there were two young ladies that came to visit me. They brought balloons and flowers and tried to perk up my spirit. They said they would take me to a Broadway show or one of the plays, or whenever a band was playing like Glen Miller, Tommy Dorsey or Jimmy Dorsey there at one of the main theaters in town. They would also take me to a nice restaurant if I wanted to go.

So I got permission to leave the hospital the next day. We went in a taxi cab to a nice restaurant. It was the first restaurant food I had since I had left the States. It was good.

Then we went to see Guy Lombardo and his Royal Canadians at one of the major movie houses that was converted into a ballroom where people could dance and listen to this music. Of course, being in a wheelchair, I sat there and enjoyed it because it was getting away from the normal routine at the hospital.

One of the gals wasn't much of a lady as she had a very filthy mouth. Every other word was a cuss word. Of course, I didn't agree with that. I felt like a woman should never cuss or swear. I really didn't want to associate with her, so I told her one day not to come anymore. She got mad and said, "Ok, if that's the way you want it." But the other continued to come every day and help me.

Finally after six months at the hospital and another major surgery ... they had to reopen the wound and do all the things they had to do, They then told me I was being discharged from the Marine Corps. I was getting a medical survey for disability. I was still not walking on that leg, and I asked them about that. They said that the Veteran's Administration would take over my case.

I don't know if you know anything about the VA, but when I went to them after I was discharged, they weren't too sympathetic toward veterans. Remember now, you're on the east coast ... and on the east coast they did not yet feel the effects of the war in the South Pacific. Our involvement in the European war had not really gotten into full swing yet ... but that would change as time went by.

Going back to my discharge ... they had me go up before a medical survey board of about eight officers. I had petitioned them to stay in the service, and be transferred to the clerical division to where I could maybe do typing and record filing and those sort of things ... hoping that when I got well, I could go back to another line of service.

I wanted to be a baker or cook. But they said, "No, with a war on we need to send the disabled veterans out of the service and into civilian life." So I was turned down and was ordered to leave ... but I refused to leave the hospital.

I went before the board again and pleaded my case. They turned me down, and this time they said this was the last appeal I could make. They said that by the 30th of the month I should be out the front gate as a civilian. If I wasn't I would be arrested, as I was now a civilian, and I had my discharge papers in my hand.

That was a very sad day for me for I had enlisted in the Marines to be a Marine, and I didn't want to leave the Marine Corps. But they left me little or no choice.

After receiving my mustering out pay which was $300, I went out the gate with another discharged Marine who had a bad hand. He had been shot in the hand and didn't have much use of it. He was going to Pennsylvania, and I was headed for Connecticut.

As we took the cab down toward Grand Central Station, we were feeling very sorry for ourselves. So we decided when we got out of the cab that we wouldn't go home right away. We would visit a couple of bars and maybe get to the place where we would feel better about ourselves.

Well you know alcohol. Sometimes you will steam the brain to where you don't think clearly, and this is what happened to us. As we made the rounds of the nightclubs with $300 in our pocket and not eating anything, I apparently passed out.

The next morning I woke up in the Astor Hotel. In bed beside me was a Canadian WAC. I had a terrible headache and hangover. I asked her, "What are you doing here? And what am I doing here?" She said, "Well, I happened to be in that last bar when I saw you pass out. My girlfriend and I brought your buddy and you to the Astor Hotel and got a couple of rooms. I'm here to help you. I happen to be a nurse.

So I thank God that even in my stupidity He was there to look after me. After we had breakfast and lunch, we thanked them and said goodbye. They headed back to Canada, and we went our separate ways.

The other Marine went on to Pennsylvania, and I went to Connecticut. When I got there, I took a cab to my house. My mother was quite surprised. She didn't expect me. She was very thankful that I was there. I was still on crutches, and so I tried to use my leg, putting it over an old fashioned brass bed rail and pushing on it and bending it every day to exercise it.

I got so that I didn't really care if I put some weight on it. Apparently, when I did, I broke a piece of bone off in my leg, so I called the Brooklyn Naval Hospital. They wanted to do the operation rather than the VA, even though I was a discharged veteran. They asked me to take the train back, and they would have a nurse meet me there.

So I went back to the hospital again for leg surgery where they removed this piece of bone that apparently was causing the infection in the leg. As I began to walk and to use a cane, I met some war brides that were there. They were very lonely and were always looking for companionship.

Many of the servicemen there who had been wounded enjoyed their company. I was in that hospital about a week and then went home again. I had not yet registered with the VA so they did not know that I was available for their care.

HOPE FOR WOUNDED WARRIORS

CHAPTER 7: REEMPLOYMENT & A BAD MARRIAGE

I started to look for work, and I went to a company that was a machine shop. I thought maybe I could sit on a stool at one of the screw machines that was making guns for the war effort. I could use my arms and hands, and I thought I could be taught a trade.

I didn't realize that with my spine still twisted a bit that I would have paralyzing strokes. I would fall off the stool, and they would have to come, stop the machine, and help me back on the stool. Management didn't think that would work out too well, so they let me go after thirty days.

I sat at home wondering what was my future, and what would I do? In the meanwhile my girlfriend had called on the phone. I had been engaged to a young lady, and she was training to be a nurse when I left for the service. We wrote lots of letters.

It was a great romance by mail, but when I got home, she came to the house one night. She handed me back the diamond engagement ring and said she didn't believe she could be married to a cripple. Being a nurse, she didn't think she loved me that much, so she wanted to break the engagement and told me I was free to date anybody I wanted to.

I was very angry and upset, as I was hoping and praying that someday she would be my wife. I had a terrible temper at that time … (God has since "tempered" me.) In my anger I threw the ring into the furnace and watched it melt down in the hot coals. That was the end of that relationship.

71

General Electric was in Bridgeport, Connecticut, and they were in a war effort and making radar for the Navy. I felt this was an opportunity that I could go to work for them. I took the train up there every day and went to personnel.

After the first application was filled out, the personnel director would see me come through the door, and she would say, "I don't have anything for you." I went back five days one week, two days the next week, every day at the same time and asked for work.

Finally, I must have broke them down, and one of the job supervisors came down and said, "Anyone who is as persistent as you," (I was still in uniform at that time as you were allowed to wear the uniforms during the war effort) and said, "we will try to teach you radar inspection at the end of the line when the radars come off the line. Your job will be to inspect them for flaws, rough edges, and things of that sort, and calibrate them. That will be your job and you can either stand or sit." So that was an ideal job for me.

But you know, the funny thing about it was, I never got to do that job. Ernie Hobbs, who was the manager of the department, was a good friend, and he was a very influential man in the community. I liked him and he seemed to like me, so we got along real well.

What happened was, when General Electric found out that I was a disabled war veteran and still using a cane, they decided that maybe they could use me in "war talks" for war bond sales and Red Cross blood drives. I said, "Sure, I'll be glad to do that." Of course, they would have me on the regular payroll.

Every job shift that came on, they would take the employees off the job and would meet in a large recreation hall, and I would give the talk about my war experiences, how I was wounded.

They raised over a million dollars in war bonds, and I don't know how many thousands of gallons of blood were donated because of my stories to the people of the General Electric Company. There were three shifts, and I spoke at all three of them regularly, because there were those who asked me to come back.

Little did I know that word got back to Washington, D.C. Henry Morgenthau Jr. made a trip up to New York City, and they invited me to participate in a War Bond rally at Carnegie Hall in New York City. There were hundreds of people there in the audience. They had a young lady come and sing "My Bill" to me while I was on the platform. It was very touching.

Then Morgenthau, the Secretary of the Treasury, came up on the stage and awarded me a Citation of Appreciation for services rendered in behalf of the War Finance Program. (Dated March 7, 1944) I was very touched. I thanked him, and we had pictures taken. I went home after that to G.E., and I stayed there for about a year, still walking with a cane and limping badly.

Meanwhile, the gal who had often visited me in the Brooklyn Naval Hospital with her foul-mouthed girl friend wrote me a letter and said she wanted to see me and talk to me. Would I come to New York and meet her at a certain place in Flushing. So I said, "Yes," and I took the train down to New York and went to Flushing and met with her.

She said she was pretty enamored with me and would like to marry me. I didn't love her and I really don't think she loved me. I think it was more pity than it was love.

73

But I was lonely and I needed somebody. I was unhappy with the home situation ... living with my step-father and my mother. I really didn't care for him too much. I didn't like living there. I felt like a fifth wheel, so we talked about getting married.

Soon after, she came up to New Haven, and we had our wedding in the Adventist Church across town. One of her girlfriends loaned her a wedding gown. She used it, and we had a large wedding with the Adventist minister administering the vows. You must remember that at this point in time I wasn't saved. I had backslid away from the Lord. He hadn't called me yet to ministry.

We hadn't been married for six months when she began to badger me to move to Ohio. Her mother and dad lived in Tennessee, and it was only a half-day's drive from Dayton down to Cokeville, Tennessee, where her folks were with her brothers and sisters.

Finally, I gave in and left General Electric. We were living in a furnished flat so we didn't have anything but our suitcases. We stayed with her uncle, her aunt, and two young ladies ... one was 13 and the other 15. We spent about a year with them while I tried to find work. Meanwhile, my wife found work as a teller in one of the branch banks in the area.

I remember going up to the Unemployment Office. I went up an applied for a job. I said, "I can't do much because I'm still limping around on a cane, but maybe you would have some kind of work." The lady adjusted her glasses, looked up the job listings, and asked where I was from. I answered, "I'm from Connecticut."

She says, "Have you ever thought about going back home and looking for a job?" I looked at her and asked, "Why?" She says, "Really, jobs here are for Ohio people, not for Connecticut people."

I was so upset and I said, "You know, I fought for every state in the Union. I just didn't fight for Connecticut. I fought for you here in Ohio and every other state. I think that you are wrong in your thinking." And she says, "Well, everyone is entitled to their opinion. I don't think there is any work here for you." So I left. I was really dejected.

Many days passed where I was living in the pity-party. I was so sorry for myself that I couldn't find work. They had started my pension at $10 per month, which of course you couldn't live on that. It was just a pittance really. So I went downtown in Dayton one day, and I was sitting on the courthouse steps. Matter of fact, the post office was right across the street.

Dayton wasn't a large city. It had a population of maybe 150,000 - 200,000 people at that time. I sat there watching the traffic and people go by. All of a sudden the thought occurred to me, "Why don't you apply at the post office?" It's a federal office, and maybe they will have some kind of work for you to do.

I went up to the postmaster's office and rapped on the door, went in, and sat down. I asked him for a job, and he looked at me and said to me, "You got quite a disability there. You've got a cane, and you are limping. I don't know. Where did you get injured?" I told him, "I just came back from the war. I'm a war casualty." He said, "Well, I would like to hire you. I've got lots of clerical jobs open that you could do and maybe someday if you want to be a carrier, we could transfer you over to be a carrier."

But he said, "The law says that anyone who hires a person that is disabled, if their disability interferes with their job, then they have the right to sue the company they are working for, and so that says you could sue us if that disability of yours should collapse on you and cause a lot of headaches.

You'll have to get a waiver from a doctor saying you are no longer in the service, and are being hired by the Treasury Dept. and not the Veterans Administration. You give us that waiver and we'll put you to work on a temporary basis."

Well I went to all the doctors in town ... at least I called them on the phone and told them my case, and everyone turned me down. But I told each one of them who I was and my telephone number and where I lived. They said, "Ok, if we change our minds we'll call you."

In the meantime we were living at my wife's uncle's house. We saw Christmas through, but it wasn't a very merry Christmas because one of the teen girls was in conflict with her parents.

The oldest daughter wanted roller skates and her mom and dad didn't think it was too wise to give her skates because of the traffic on the streets and sidewalks. So they didn't give her skates, and she became upset on Christmas morning and stomped out of the room and went up to her room and slammed the door.

She didn't come out to eat Christmas dinner with us. She never seemed to forget that roller skates were the only thing she wanted for Christmas and they denied her that. It surely shows how one person's bitterness can impact everyone in the home.

One day while I was there at my wife's uncle's house, the phone rang, and it was a doctor across town. He said that he was retiring from his practice, and he would sign a waiver. If I would come in he would give me a statement of my condition and that the post office would not be held responsible.

I took that into the postmaster and he said, "Ok, you're hired. What can you do?" I said, "I want to be a carrier." He said, "Well, I'm afraid that's awful difficult." I said, "Listen, you teach me what to do. I'm on a cane but I'll show you that I can deliver the mail."

So he said, "All right. We'll teach you how to sort mail, and we'll assign you to a route wherever we can. If there is one open, we'll put you on that and see what happens."

Back in those days they had the little three wheeled carts that you push around. I had one of those locked up in a storage box out on this route. I took the bus out; got the cart out of the storage box; hung my bag on it; and away I went. I limped up to every house with my cane and did my tour of duty as required; put the cart back in the box and hopped on a bus to go back to the post office.

I worked that route for about three months, and I noticed one thing that started to happen. My back felt better, and I noticed that I didn't need the cane to walk with as often. What was happening, the exercise was good therapy for my knee and my leg. It was really paying off both ways.

After three months the postmaster came to me and said that they are holding civil service exams on Saturday. If I would come in, I could take the test. If I passed it, I would become a temporary regular carrier until I was assigned to a permanent route, and then I would become a regular carrier and my seniority in service would start.

So I took the exam and passed it, and was assigned to a route on the north part of the city. It so happened it was just about maybe a quarter of a mile from my house. That worked out real well.

I now was able to drive, and we had an old broken down car. Usually, I would take the bus to the post office and back home because it was only three blocks to the bus stop. Only in the case of down-pouring rain did I ever need to use the car.

Meanwhile my wife would walk three blocks to her bank so it wasn't too bad a deal. Well, I got tired of living with her uncle, so one Sunday afternoon, while we were out driving, we noticed a "For Sale" sign on a big two-story house situated on two acres of land about a mile and half from where we were staying.

It was an ugly looking house with clabber boards on the outside. It hadn't been painted for years. Come to find out, the house was a log house made of chestnut logs. It had been plastered on the inside, and the clabber board put on the outside.

That didn't make too good of a situation because the field mice would get in there under the clabber board in the winter time. They would make their nests in the walls. They couldn't get into the house because of the thick plaster, but they would run up and down, and it was very nerve wracking to hear them scratching and moving about.

We bought the house on a land contract that didn't require any money down. The man that owned it was an attorney at law so he said, "Make your payments to me each

78

month and at the end of your contract you'll own the house."
But technically, he gave us a copy of the deed with our name
on it, and it would be ours once the note was paid off. It
wasn't too much ... something around six or seven thousand
dollars. Remember ... that was back in 1945.

So we moved in. It had the old fashioned electric
lights that hung out of the ceiling with a little switch on them
... nothing modern at all. The heat came from an oil floor
heater that was under ground. There was no basement,
though somebody had dug a hole under the house to put the
furnace in. That was about the way it was.

The house was sitting on two acres of ground, so we
sold off an acre for $1000, and that helped us to manage our
debt and get by. Our bedroom was upstairs. There was one
bedroom upstairs and one down. There were no light
switches on the wall. A wire with a light bulb hung from the
ceiling. The light socket had an off and on switch. When you
came into the room, you had to turn on the switch on the light
socket, so you had to use a flashlight to go upstairs.

They said the house was haunted by a ghost. That's
why he said they couldn't sell it to anybody. At times you
could hear ... it sounded like someone dropped a bowling ball
at the top of the stairs and it bounced all the way down every
step to the bottom. You could walk over to the stairway and
there would be nothing there, but you heard the noise.

It didn't bother me any because I don't believe in
ghosts. So whatever the noise was, it was an acceptable thing.
At that time we had chickens, rabbits, ducks and a little bit of
everything. It was a mini-farm I guess. We had plenty of eggs
and chickens to eat ... ducks and duck eggs.

We enjoyed being there, but after a while she wanted a permanent place for her parents. They lived in a house in Tennessee that was on about 5 acres of ground. They slept on straw mattresses and heated their house by fireplaces and a cook stove in the kitchen. Coal oil lamps were used to read by.

It was a real rural Tennessee home in the hills. Most of the roads were not paved. There was only one paved road to Livingstone which was about ten miles away. It ran to Cokeville which was about 7-8 miles the other way. All the rest of the roads were dirt.

My father-in-law owned the general store not too far away from the house they lived in. They had a tin roof. It was very cold and airy. You could see the outside light come in between the boards around the building. It was a real country type rural cheap inexpensive type home that someone had thrown up.

He sold the business and went to Detroit to work in the car industry when the war broke out. Now he was retired, so they wanted a place for him to live permanently up in Dayton where there was a little more civilization with stores, doctors and what have you.

So we started to look for another house close to the post office. I was driving a 1937 Ford coupe that would really only seat two people. In the winter it had a gasoline heater off of the carburetor. I drove it to work every day. The wife wasn't working at that time. She didn't get on at the bank until we bought the house in Salem Heights.

We found two old houses constructed before 1940, both on one lot. The back house was a little three room cottage. We lived in the front house that included two

80

bedrooms on the first floor. Upstairs under the roof was a large room that ran from one side of the house to the other. The place was heated by an oil furnace in the full basement.

So we sold the rural home with the ducks and chickens, got a G.I. Loan from the bank, and bought the house with no money down. We moved into the front house, and the in-laws, her mother and dad, moved into the cottage in the back.

It was close to the bus line and just a couple of blocks from the big shopping center. We called them big back in those days. It was actually a strip mall with a furniture store, a department store, a drug store and a grocery store. That's about all, but it was enough to take care of the people in that area. Across the street was the large golf course where they would play the PGA tournament in Dayton. Not far down Salem Ave. you find the University of Dayton.

While we were there my wife started a "regimen" of shoplifting. My use of the word "regimen" may surprise you, but the dictionary says it's a "systematic plan of action."

I didn't realize it at the time, but she really developed a system. Although it did seem strange that she would come home with rings on her fingers and jewelry on her neck. I would ask her where she got it and she would say, "Oh, I put it on the charge card."

At that time she was managing the money so I didn't really pay any attention. Can you imagine, back in those days I started in at the post office at 65 cents per hour? Gradually I worked myself up to 89 cents per hour. That was good money back in 1945.

I remember very clearly. I was trying to make extra money, so I took on a part time job selling dinner ware. It was supposed to be break resistant. I went into the drug store. I had a box of it in my mail bag. While I had lunch I would set it up on the counter. People who had an interest would come by and ask about it. I would tell them they could have a service of eight for x amount of money. It was a pretty set of china.

Stupid me, I told them it was "non-breakable" instead of "break resistant". I didn't realize what I was saying because there is no china that is non-breakable. It is called break-resistant because if you put it in the oven and bake with it, it won't crack or break.

One day a lady says, "If it's non-breakable drop it on the floor." I dropped a plate and it broke in a million pieces. I was so embarrassed I didn't know what to say. The waitress came out and swept it up because we were there at the lunch counter in the drug store.

My wife had had an affair in the house where we had lived. When I was out, an old friend from Tennessee came. She told me about it a long time after it happened. I don't know, maybe I thought it just gave me carte blanche to get even with her by having an affair also.

My neighbor, who was not very happy with her spouse ... a very nice lady ... we used to watch for each other to go out to the trash burner. In those days you could burn trash in a big barrel in the back of your property as long as you were careful, and it didn't get out of hand.

She would watch for me to go out, and then she would take her trash out, and we would stand there and talk, embrace and have a kiss or two. That's as far as it went for that time.

Her husband would go bowling, and she would pull the blinds open and do a little dance there to entice me. Of course I'm human, and at that time I wasn't a Christian, and I fell for it. I knew when her husband wasn't there, and I would go over, and we would have a love session. I would come home, and no one knew the difference, because my wife was out shopping or something. So we had quite an affair going.

One time her husband came home early, and I was in the bedroom. She stuck me into the basement and told her husband I was in the basement looking for a hammer as I didn't have one. So he came downstairs and found it for me. It was close. We nearly got caught. Then after that I thought it was time to cool it. She was an awfully nice person but very lonely. Those things do happen when you are not a Christian.

I recall one time when I was carrying mail. There was a real violent rainstorm, and I went into a place of business. If there was nobody in the store, I would go back into the office with the mail. Here this owner was with his secretary sitting on his lap. He was doing things that I wouldn't mention out loud.

The secretary happened to be the wife of a mail carrier at the post office. She jumped off his lap, of course, when I showed up, and she asked me not to tell her husband as she didn't want to wreck her marriage. This affair had been going on a long time, but I never revealed it to him. He told me one time while I was talking to him that they were having marital problems and that his wife wanted a divorce.

Not too long after that, I became very ill. I started bleeding from the rectum. There was a hospital on my mail route. It was run by Catholic Charities. I went in and mentioned what was happening to me, so a nurse said I should immediately go to a doctor and have it cared for because it could be cancer.

So I made an appointment with a referral she gave me to a colon doctor. Come to find out that I had an acute case of colitis. He started me on a medication, but I didn't seem to get much better. So one day he said, "I want to talk to your wife. Can you bring her in?" I said, "Well, if I can get her in, I will."

It took quite a bit of persuasion to get her to go, but finally she consented. First thing the doctor said was, "You know that you are responsible for what's wrong with your husband." She looked at him and said, "What are you talking about?" He told her to quit browbeating him and quit badgering him and being belligerent to him and treating him like he is your enemy.

She said, "What? How do you know I do those things?" He said, "Because the condition he's got of ulcerated colitis, 99% comes from a nagging wife. I assume that she is fully responsible for her husband's condition." She got angry and slammed out of the office.

When I came home, she really chewed me out about what the doctor had said. But of course, she didn't change her ways. She stayed the same ... still shoplifting ... still having affairs that I learned about later. Meanwhile, I was no saint either. I just have to confess that I am amazed at how patient God has been with people like me across those years.

CHAPTER 8: BACK TO THE LORD

I worked at the post office in Dayton for eighteen years as a carrier. One night as I was going upstairs to the bedroom to sleep, a little inner voice said, "Don't turn on the light." My wife had quit going to church, but I was still attending, though I was backslid and away from the Lord.

The inner voice said, "Don't turn on the light. Just go up to your bedroom, open your Bible, and it will fall open to where I want you to read." So I said to myself, "OK" and I opened my Bible. It was at the place where it said to cast in the sickle because the harvest is ripe.

The Lord said, "I want you to go down to the Bible College tomorrow and apply. I said, "Lord, I don't have any money, and I'm not in any shape to go to Bible College. Besides, my heart isn't right."

The Lord said, "I want you to go down and talk to the Dean." So I went down and talked to the Dean, and I told him that I didn't have any money and couldn't go ... and that I wasn't really in the place..." He said, "Well, I think the Lord will straighten your heart out for you if you start attending Bible College because you'll be convicted, and one night you'll give your heart back to Him."

So I said, "What are we going to do about the money situation?" He said, "I'm going to let you go a month. If no money comes in for your support in a month after the school prays for you every day, then I'm going to drop you, and we'll have to believe it wasn't the Lord's call. If it's the Lord's call, then you will have money to come to take care of it.

A little after a month there was more money than you could believe. People from the church, when the announcement was made that I wanted to go to Bible College and needed money ... money came in. My brother, he even sent money. I had enough to go to Bible College at night.

The Dean was right. One night I was up in the prayer loft of this three story church. The whole roof of it was a skylight of stained glass. As the moon shone down through the stained glass and lit up the altar, I made a commitment to the Lord that I wanted to come back and be His child again.

That night, as I was praying for guidance, I had a vision. The Lord held out His hand to me across a river. On His side it was covered with flowers. He said, "If you take My hand now, you will come home with Me. What is your answer?" I replied, "No, Lord, I have work to do for You. I am willing to stay here and do it."

You know, after I went to Bible College and got my Minister's License, my wife began to give me trouble. She didn't want me in the ministry. She hated the ministry and hated me talking about it.

I didn't intend to quit the post office. I wanted to be a youth pastor in a new church that started up on the east side of town. I helped the pastor take orange crates and put boards across them for seats. We made a make-shift altar rail out of boxes and a pulpit out of orange crates and covered it with a cloth. We made do, and we opened up a store-front church. It's surprising how many people came.

He would preach every Sunday, but once in a while he would give me a chance. So one Sunday I preached on the Second Coming of Christ. Afterwards I held an altar call, and

I asked for anyone that wanted to give their heart to the Lord to come forward.

A woman slipped out of her seat. She was about maybe 20-21. She came and knelt at the make-shift altar. She began to cry and scream and to tear her hair out and tear her clothes. She just went into a terrible fit. The pastor said to me, "Where's the oil? Get it and we're going to get down and rebuke this demon that is possessing her. She'll be all right. She'll finally come through, she'll pray through."

So we anointed her, and all of a sudden, a calm came over her, and she prayed through. Later on after she became a regular attendee at the church, she told us that she had been a street prostitute. Just by chance she had heard the singing, and she stumbled in and sat down to hear the message.

When she heard the message, she came forward, but the devil didn't want to turn loose of her. He began to cause her to scream, tear her hair and tear her clothes. When we rebuked Satan in the name of Jesus, this demon came out and left her free. She got a regular job and eventually married a nice man.

As I carried the mail route, I carried the message of the gospel with me. I remember one house that I went to. The lady's husband had passed away just a week or so before. I had a registered letter for her so I rang the doorbell.

She came and signed for the letter,. Then she said, "Won't you come in for a cup of coffee? It's cold out there." I said, "No, I'm running late". But the Holy Spirit was prompting me to talk to her about the Lord. I wouldn't go in. So she signed and closed the door.

I felt so guilty because the Lord really convicted me. I prayed for another opportunity to witness. So the next time she had to sign for a registered letter and invited me in for a cup of coffee, I went into her kitchen.

I told her that I was a stamp collector. She showed me stacks and stacks of plate blocks of stamps. One room was just full of stacks of sheets of different stamps. He husband had been a dealer in stamps. She offered me a sheet from every one of those packages, but I didn't take it. I asked her if she knew Jesus and she said, "No, but I've heard about him. Tell me about Him." So as we had coffee I shared the gospel, and she accepted the Lord.

There was another couple on my route. I usually got there about lunch time. One day I went in and had apple pie and coffee with them. I ate my lunch with them as I always carried it with me in the bag. Every day they would have me stop.

I carried a little Testament with me, and I would read them a scripture and talk to them about it. She was a Lutheran but never attended church. He was an atheist and didn't believe in God. I recall they had a little three year old girl. For over a year I would stop every day to eat lunch and share the gospel.

One night when I was home, very late ... about 2 or 3 o'clock in the morning, the phone rang. I picked it up. Carl, the atheist husband, was on the phone. He was screaming at me, "I just accepted the Lord. I just accepted the Lord. We were going through Arizona. We saw a tent revival and we stopped and went in, and the Lord convicted me. I gave my heart to the Lord and so did the wife and our little girl. I wanted you to know because I couldn't contain the news so I phoned you."

Later on, when they came home, I stopped for coffee, and she had a homemade apple pie. It was a time of rejoicing with that family. His daughter had leukemia but God touched her and she fully recovered.

One time I was asked to preach at a particular church. Being a young, energetic youth pastor, I accepted. I preached a message that would raise the hair on the back of your neck. I mean, I preached that if you don't give your heart to God, you are on your way to Hell. Then I had an altar call and many people came forward to accept Christ.

After the service a couple of the elders of the church, including the minister, cornered me as I started to leave, and they said, "You see that door? Don't ever come back through it again. We don't like your way of preaching, and we don't have altar calls in this church. We don't have people make decisions for Christ in this church. If you think you're going to get away with it, next time, you're mistaken, because there isn't going to be a next time."

I got that opportunity through a printer who was on my mail route. He was attending that church, and he thought it would be nice if I would come and preach a nice quiet encouraging message. It was encouraging, but not to their liking ... but the printer still gave me stationery and calling cards at no cost to me.

I was going to be ordained at the college. I asked my wife to go to graduation with me. After the graduation service there was to be the ordination service. I didn't realize how much she opposed my wanting to be a pastor.

Nevertheless, she agreed to come to the graduation. She thought I was getting a religious education certificate. When they called me up as Reverend William Lentsch, a

Licensed Minister of the Gospel, her face got red ... white ... and then almost purple, she was so angry. She up and stormed out of the church.

I told them at that time that I wouldn't take ordination because of the conditions at home, and I didn't think it would be the right thing to do. So I turned down ordination at that time.

CHAPTER 9: MOVE TO CALIFORNIA

Seeing that the situation at home wasn't getting any better with more and more stuff that she was bringing into the house that she had stolen, I decided it might be a good idea to get out of the state of Ohio and move to California. I liked San Diego pretty well when I was there in the Naval Hospital. I liked the climate and the city and I thought, well, I'm going to see if I can get a transfer to the post office in California.

So I wrote to the postmaster in West Covina. Why West Covina? After I had put an ad in the "Letter Carrier" magazine for a mutual trade, a carrier from there wrote to me. He wanted to come to Chillicothe, Ohio, which is not too far from Dayton. He was willing to trade if the post master there would accept him and the one in West Covina would accept me.

So I wrote the post master and told him who I was and explained all about my carrier service. At that time I had about 13 years in the Post Office. He said that he would approve it, but he reminded me that I would go on the bottom of the seniority list ... same as a new man starting out.

The only difference it really would make was the fact that when you are a senior carrier, you get a better choice of routes. The man coming in does not get the route that the other carrier left. They put that route up for bid, and any carrier can write his name next to the route if he wants it. Then the man with highest seniority gets that route. So I said that was alright with me. That was all unbeknown to my wife. She didn't realize what I was doing.

They accepted him in Chillicothe, Ohio, and so the deal was made, and I had to make the transfer. I had a month or two to sell out and make the move. I told her one night that we were moving to California. She wasn't too happy with that decision, but she got her sister to agree that she would move out there if we would move out there.

That kind of made it easier for her to make the move. So we went ahead, packed up all our stuff, and got a large moving company to move us. I came out here a week or two early and found a rental in La Puente on Francisquito Avenue. We moved into that rental. It was a nice home on a quiet street. We moved in, and I went to work for the post office in West Covina.

The only route they had open was one with about 250 apartment units, plus some business, and some residential. It was a total of about 350 stops. I learned the route, and I had to learn how to ride a bicycle all over again as they used them to go door to door delivering mail. Of course, in an apartment complex, you deliver mail to four lock boxes. You unlock the top and drop the mail in. It takes a long time.

So I went to the manager of the apartments. I mentioned that he could put in all of the mail boxes so they could be reached from his office. The boxes would be on the outside but you could drop down the front side in his office to deliver the mail. This way, he would have better control over who went to the boxes as they were having trouble with people stealing the mail.

They agreed, and soon they tore out one wall of his office and put in 250 lock boxes with the apartment numbers on them. The people weren't really too happy with that as they had to come up to the office to get their mail, but it did stop the stealing. That was a real feather in my cap, plus I could make one stop for 250 apartments. That was a great move.

I recall before the change of boxes, when I was still carrying into the apartments there was a little three year old boy in diapers one spring. It must have been about March and it was cold. All he had on was a diaper. He was as mean as a barrel of snakes.

When he would see me coming, he would run and jump up on my back, start biting me on my ears, kick me in the stomach, and give me a lot of trouble. Finally I couldn't take much more of it, so I went to his mother and complained. He had no father. So she says, "Boys will be boys at that age, you know. You can put up with it."

So I went to the post master and told him what was going on. He put a stop order on all mail to the apartments until that little boy was taken care of. People got all upset and they went to the manager. The manager went to her and said, "If you don't keep the child inside when the carrier is here, you won't get any mail and neither will anybody else. We've got a lot of unhappy people here. So she moved out and that solved that problem.

There was an egg ranch on my route. That lady used to give me two dozen eggs every week. She appreciated my service. I would take the mail to her door. She was a nice person and I enjoyed that.

There was also a drive-in restaurant, an IN & OUT hamburger place. I used to eat there and at a drug store that would let me eat my lunches at their lunch counter. I could run a tab at the drug store and that worked out real well for me.

93

I did have a problem when it rained. It was pretty hard to ride a bicycle. It was five miles to my route from the post office. But you know, in Southern California it doesn't rain all that much, so you put up with it. We had good rain gear.

One day I happened to be driving down Puente Avenue in West Covina, and I saw this house for sale. I took down the phone number, and I called them. I told them that I would like to go through it. I told my wife that I would like to go through it.

It had a quarter of an acre of land behind it and it was rich land. In fact, the oil company came and checked if there was any oil beneath it. There was a small pool of oil, but not enough to make it worthwhile to draw a pipeline to it, so they just never worked it. I got the royalty rights to it, but it never produced.

I had a huge garden on that quarter acre ... all kinds of fruit trees, all kinds of vegetables, plus rhubarb. You just name it. I used to can up about 250 jars of peaches every year ... plus pears, avocados, jams and jellies.

I was in the kitchen every fall working real hard putting up all these homemade canned fruits and vegetables. I used to can beets, carrots, Swiss chard and spinach. My father-in-law used to come out and stay with us in the winter time with the mother-in-law. He would turn the garden by shovel and hand plow. We had a nice garden.

We also raised three nice turkeys one time ... but I couldn't kill them. They were almost like pets. I raised three or four nice big ducks too. I couldn't kill them either, but I finally sold them to a poultry house or traded them for some dressed chickens. I didn't feel like I had lost too much, although, the turkeys dressed out around 25 pounds.

I could never get my wife to go to church. Once in while the father-in-law would go with me. You know, you can take the hill-billy out of the hills, but you couldn't change them. They lived all their lives in the hills.

He chewed tobacco. He had an old coffee can to spit in, but he often missed, so it kept the rug stained. He cussed and swore. It was a difficult time. Every weekend he wanted to go somewhere and we had to drive them.

Meanwhile, the wife continued with her shop lifting habits. I didn't realize how bad they were. She had opened up charge accounts at all the major department stores and had them filled right up to the limit.

I had three mortgages on the house, and I had to find another job. I got off work at the post office at three o'clock, and at four o'clock, I would go to work as a janitor for a lens company where they used to make lenses for a telescope and other devices. I would clean the offices, restrooms, and parts of the factory that were not working at night. I would be done at 2:00 o'clock in the morning. I would go home, flop into bed, and get up again at 5 o'clock to be at the post office at six.

I did this five days a week and then drove the in-laws everywhere. We went to the Indio Fair and Orange County Fair. We went to the Los Angeles County Fair. We went to every shopping mall and every center you could think of. We went to Palm Springs a couple of times, the Salton Sea ... all over. But we never did come to San Diego. I don't know why. The furthest we ever got was Laguna Beach. We went down there several times, spent the day, had dinner, and then we would come home.

I didn't have much money. I was pretty broke because the post office didn't pay much at that time. My wife, she was working at a bank. She didn't make much money either. By the time we paid all the major bills coming due, we couldn't pay them all. They were piling up on us.

Things were getting worse. We were getting phone calls from the creditors ... being harassed night and day by mail and by phone calls. Life got to be real trying. I had three mortgages and still could not pay all the bills.

Little did I know that every time we went into a department store, she would take whatever she wanted, whether it be a set of towels, shoes, dresses, blouses, skirts, coats, and she would have a pair of scissors and she would clip off the tags. At that time they didn't have the alarm devices the way they do today. She would slip a coat on and another coat over it. Then she would go into the changing room and put on a couple of skirts and blouses.

She began to pilfer silverware and the stuff would pile up at the house. I kept screaming at her and warning that I was going to call the police. But she said I would never do it because I was a Christian man. I threatened divorce, and she said that I would never do it because I didn't believe in divorce. Things just went from bad to worse.

I began to buy trunks, and she would fill the trunks full. When the garage got full and we didn't have hardly any room to get to the washer and dryer, we had to lease a storage unit in a rental building. We stored all of the boxes and barrels and trunks there. She had no idea how much stuff she was stealing.

I recall one day we were in Montgomery Ward. She was on a knitting gig. She had just learned to knit and needed balls of yarn. So she would take a Ward's bag from a previous purchase, fold it up under her coat, then she would get in the area where the yarn was. She would pick out the skeins she wanted by numbers and then she would open the bag and fill the bag full. So if anyone saw her they would think she was carrying a purchase.

One day a security guard was alerted by a clerk. He watched her. As we went out the door, she handed me the bag. As soon as we went out of the store, he grabbed us by the scuff of the neck and hauled us back into the store.

He brought us down to his security office and asked, "What do we do with you two?" I said, "I'm not guilty. All I did was carry the bag." I didn't carry it because I knew she stole anything, I didn't pay any attention. I happen to be in another part of the store. He said, "OK, we'll let you go. But I don't know what I'll do with her."

I lied to him saying, "As far as I know, it's her first offense. As far as I'm concerned, she'll never do it again if I can do anything about it." So he says, "Well, OK, but remember don't ever come back in this store again because I've got a picture. You'll be up on the employee's bulletin board. The next time she does this, we'll arrest her on the charge of shoplifting."

So she was barred from the store in Covina. She could never go into that Wards again. But she didn't need to because she went into Sears, and Penney's, and other Wards stores out of the area. She was having a field day with everything she was buying and stealing. She didn't stop.

It got so bad with me working two jobs ... and driving them everywhere. I thought, maybe before I retire, if I could get her out of the area where all the stores are and get her up in the mountains, get her away, maybe she would stop her nonsense, because if ever she got caught, she would wind up in jail. I knew that and that I might just wind up going to jail with her.

There was an opening on a mail route up in the mountains above Malibu in a community that needed a rural letter carrier. I was driving the 1938 Ford to work, and I thought maybe I might transfer up there and carry mail to all the rural boxes. I wouldn't have to get out of the car. Just deliver them right from the car, so I put in for a transfer.

That was one of the biggest mistakes of my life. When you go from regular carrier service to rural, you go to an altogether different division of service. The pay schedules are different. The situations are different. The internal system is different. I didn't realize that and neither did I check into it. I was so distraught at the time that I thought anything to get away from what is going on would be better.

It was a long drive. I had to drive all the way from West Covina through Santa Monica, up to Malibu, and on up into the mountains. It was a very long commute, but I felt that it was what I wanted to do, so I transferred. It was quite a different setup all together.

I had to leave the house about six o'clock to beat the traffic. I was going across the traffic so it wasn't so bad. Coming home, I would be coming home about 3 o'clock, and the traffic wouldn't pick up yet so heavy. My route, when it was done, I was done for the day. I didn't hit a time clock like we did as a carrier. I didn't have to worry about what time I got there or got done. The traffic would more or less regulate my comings and goings.

I wasn't there more than a couple months when I looked for a house and found one. Then on one Sunday I took her father and mother and her up to look at the house. It was a beautiful home in the mountains, and I felt I could swing the payments. I could sell my house and move up there. Then I would be right close to work, and it would all work out.

Well her father didn't want to go up there and be stuck in the mountains, and so he told his daughter, my wife, I'm not going up there, so don't you go up there. Well, she was afraid of her father. If you recall earlier in the story she had run away from home. And so, she would not go. So here I am stuck in a rural route way up there and they won't move. But, I stuck it out.

The name of the town was called Topanga Canyon. It was a nice rural post office. I remember one day I pulled up to the dock to load my mail. There was a little dog, a terrier. He was pretty skinny. You could see his ribs. He looked like he was starving.

It was about lunch time, and I had a baloney sandwich. I tore off a chunk and tossed it to him. He gulped that down like he hadn't eaten in a week. I threw him the rest of the sandwich, and he ate it. So I ate an apple to tide me over until I got home.

When I opened up the door to get in, he jumped in alongside of me. I said, "You can't ride with me." He growled and snarled at me. I said, "You can't go. I can't haul a dog around with me on my route," ... but he wouldn't get out. Again he snarled and snapped at me, so I shut the door and said, "Away we go." He made the route with me. He barked at every dog on the route and every car that went by ... barked at it and at everybody that came out to get their mail.

There happened to be two nudist camps on this route. It was quite an interesting place to get used to, especially when you had a registered letter that had to be signed for. After you rang the buzzer, the iron gates would open and you would go in. The gates would shut behind you.

Then you would drive up to the office and get out of the car to go into the office with the letter. Of course, everybody there is without any clothes on which was quite shocking. Over a loud speaker, they would announce the person who has to sign for it. Then you waited for them to come in.

One was a young lady who came in without any clothes on. She says, "What do you want?" I said, "You have a registered letter," so she signed for it. After I got the signature, I got in the car and turned around. Around the swimming pool there were a lot of people playing volleyball or just relaxing by the pool. I drove out and went on to finish my rounds.

When I got back to the post office, I opened the door and the dog jumped out and disappeared. I was hoping that would be the last of the dog! I don't know where he went, but the next morning he was on the dock ... waiting for me. As soon as I opened the door to load the mail, he was in the front seat ... sitting up.

So he rode with me for about two months. Finally one Friday, I was getting ready to leave. We didn't deliver mail on Saturday as it was a rural route. I opened the door to get into the car to go home, and he jumped in. I said, "You can't go with me. I'm going home." Again he put on that act of snarling at me and growling at me. He wouldn't move so I said, "O.K., I'll take you home."

He rode all the way home with me ... but when I got home, my wife wouldn't let him stay in the house. She said, "I won't have a dog in the house," so I kept him outside. Every day I fed and watered him. Every day he would get in the car with me and I had a shot-gun companion so to speak. He would ride up to Topanga Canyon with me and ride the mail route ... and go back home with me at night.

So he became "my dog." It was a wonderful thing to have a pal for the next five years. On the Fourth of July I had him locked in the house, but the noise of the fireworks was too much for him. He got out, and a car ran over him.

Then the bank decided, because my wife had carpal tunnel syndrome and she couldn't do the work at the bank, they let her go. I remember I was so angry. I went to the bank and talked to the manager. He said, "Well, we have a policy here, after you have lost so many days, we have to let you go." I said, "But she was on sick leave. She had a doctor's statement." But he said, "It doesn't make any difference. That's the orders from downtown."

So I asked for the address and on my day off I went down to the office and asked to speak to the General Manager. They introduced me to him and he asked, "What can I do for you?" I explained the situation and he said, "That's my policy. I made it and I'm going to stick with it. I don't care what the circumstances are."

I was mad! I had a temper at that time, and I was backslid from the Lord again, so I grabbed him by the shirt and tie and pulled him up to me and told him, "Some night, in an alley, you're going to meet your demise, fellow. This is not a threat, it's a warning. Don't walk in any dark alleys after you leave the building at night."

He got kind of scared and got white in the face, He said, "Well, what do you want me to do, hire her back again? I said, "No, she wouldn't work for you again. But I want a letter of recommendation. She had a spotless record, and she was up for a promotion before she had to take off for a job related injury.

I want you to write a letter to whom it may concern and recommend her highly." So he said, "It will be in the mail next week." So I went home and true to his word he sent a letter of recommendation. It wasn't the greatest, but at least it introduced her to a new bank so it wouldn't look bad on her record that she was let go.

Lo and behold, there was an opening nights downtown at another bank in the mail processing division where they processed all the checks that came in through the mail. They opened up the envelopes and processed the checks putting them into the right accounts. She did pretty well working nights in the mail division for about five years.

Meanwhile I was working two jobs days and trying to prepare the meals for the old folks. It was a very difficult task. Trying to can the harvest from the garden in the fall, I just had taken on more than I could handle. I could hardly take it anymore with bill collectors calling, phones ringing off the hook demanding payments.

She had run all the credit cards up to their limits with her spending. I was destitute. I went out and bought a gun and put it under the bed and contemplated that I would take her life and take mine too. I know that's a terrible thing. But truth of the matter is ... that's the way it was. That's what I did.

I retired from the post office and went to work in the furniture department of a national department store. She would come in and make such a crazy scene ... lying, cheating and hollering at me ... running off the customers. Management put her out of the store and told her if she walked into the store, they would have her arrested.

I left that job and went to work for a company that was opening a brand new furniture store in West Covina and hired about 30 sales people. When I went there, I had very little sales experience though I had worked some in a couple of furniture stores part time when I was in Dayton. I went ahead and entered a trailer that they had set up and got an application ... filled it out.

The General Manager of the store interviewed me. He said, "The only thing I want to hear is one word. Why do you want to work for this company?" Well, there could be a million words that one could think of, but the only thing I could think of was that I was desperate. I said, "Money. I want to make this company money." He says, "You're hired. That's the word we like to hear."

So when they had their grand opening, I went to work for them. When my wife found out that I was working there, she began to cause problems. She would come in and holler and scream at me when I was on the floor ... and embarrass me in front of 29 sales people. Finally management went to her and told her that she would be escorted by security every time she came in and so not to come in. So they forced her to stay out of the store.

I did very well in sales, though my earnings were small at the beginning until I got used to the furniture and the system. Finally, I became second, and then first, in sales which amounted to $60,000 a month in sales. That meant good paychecks for me because they paid 6% commission. I was making anywhere from $600 to $1000 a week. I began to show some signs of pulling out of the hole.

CHAPTER 10:
PATRICIA – GOD'S GIFT TO ME

I went to a psychiatrist. Patricia went with me. She was a friend that I had met at the store. She was looking for work when she came in. She applied for work and got a job in the sales department. Many times we would sit in the break room talking. I kind of told her my story in a way, and she said that she would go with me to the psychiatrist to see what could be done to change my mind from destroying my "ex" and myself.

So I went with her, and after a few hours with the psychiatrist, he said, "You don't have but one choice over the way that you have chosen (to shoot my wife and myself) ... which is not the way you should go." "The other choice is that you pack a suitcase tonight, put a note on the door that you are leaving ... and you leave." "I don't know where you can go. Maybe get an apartment or rent a room temporarily until you can get readjusted to a new place."

He knew that I needed "space" ... to get away from my wife. Otherwise, she might say something that would trigger my anger and in a rage, I would shoot her and then take my own life.

So I did as he said. That night when she went to work, I packed my suitcases and wrote her a big note with a felt pen, "I've had it up to my ears. I took you all the way to Monterrey for a two-week's vacation, Hearst's Castle and the whole bit, and you would not keep your promises to me that I wanted you to make. You said you wouldn't do the things I asked you to do."

I had four things I wanted her to do. One of them, I didn't want her folks out anymore as they were controlling her life and controlling me. Secondly, I wanted her to stop her shoplifting. Thirdly, I didn't want her to buy another stitch of clothing, or steal another stitch of clothing, or buy anything, or get anything. I said, "The garage is full. I've had to rent a storage space and that is full. I'm sick up to my neck with you."

The fourth thing was that we had lived like brother and sister all the time we were married. She treated me like a little brother and a bossy sister. That's about all our marriage amounted to, so I told her she would have to be more of a wife to me.

Well she told me she wasn't going to honor any of those wishes. So I made my decision to leave ... and I left. Patricia was good enough to give me a place to stay at her house. At least I had a place for room and board ... a place to eat and a place to sleep.

Funny little thing ... I had a dog with me, and I remember, one time, when I drove up to the house, the front door was open. Patricia had a Siamese cat. When I opened the car door, the dog jumped out and ran into the house. Boy, when that cat saw the dog, she went up the curtains and across the ceiling. It was acoustical ... so she could get her claws into it upside down. She ran across the ceiling, down the other curtains, and out the window. She was gone for over a month before she finally came back.

Patricia and I were very good friends. We enjoyed each other's company. She kept my account in a little black book. She took my paycheck each week and proceeded to pay off all of my bills. She did an unbelievable job in helping me to get my life back in order.

In the meanwhile my "ex" found out that I was staying there ... so the phone would ring constantly all hours of the night. It caused so much harassment that we had to change the phone number. Things were bad. She took a key and scratched vulgar words all over Patricia's car. She scratched them on the windows, the doors, and the top of the car. It was a horrible mess. It had to be all sanded down and painted.

While Patricia was having the car repainted, she drove her daughter's little Volkswagen. My wife did the same thing on that one with a felt pen. Fortunately, the guys from the furniture store came out, washed it down, and cleaned it off. That was the last that we had to deal with that sort of thing.

I filed for divorce in December of that year, and she didn't reject the idea. "If that's what you want, I'll take you to the cleaners. If that's what you want, that's the way it will be. I'll make my own decision on what I'll do with my life."

So I got an attorney, and he sold the house. The judge said that I would have to rent her a house and move her furniture in, so I did. I didn't get any money out of the house when I sold it because there was no equity built up in it. I had three mortgages on it, trying to pay off bills, and I owed several finance companies. I was in real dire shape.

After a year, Patricia and I became very close. We dated then, and I asked her to marry me, but she said, "No." She had had a horrible life. Her husband had cheated on her and walked out on her for another woman. He left her with two little children and wouldn't support her or the children. She said she didn't want to get married again. Well, I guess I must have asked her to marry me at least 50 times, but each time she turned me down.

A year later, after my divorce was final, I asked her again, and she said she would, so we got married. Of course, all this time I was backslid away from the Lord. I didn't tell her when I married her that I had been a minister and had had ministerial credentials with the church. I just said to myself that I was going to put this all behind me and start a new life.

One night when we were talking, she asked me about some things. Why I had such high ideals and such scruples? Why I had such a Christian attitude? I broke down and told her that I had been a minister ... that I had sent my credentials back and gotten out of the ministry because of my "ex".

She was quite taken aback because she had married a furniture salesman. She didn't know she had married a minister. But to make a long story short, she had known the Lord at one time and had gone away from Him too. So together we knelt and both gave our lives back to the Lord.

[EDITOR'S NOTE:

I visited with Bill on June 30, 2012, and asked him how he would respond if someone reading the story would ask: "What do you mean by: 'So together we knelt and both gave our lives back to the Lord?" He indicated that when he had attended those night classes at Bible School, he had learned how one develops a personal relationship with God.

It begins with a recognition that sin separates us from God. Citing Bible verses: Romans 3:23 declares, "For all have sinned, and come short of the glory of God." That is an undeniable reality.

Meanwhile Romans 6:23 gives bad news and good news. "For the wages of sin is death, but the gift of God is eternal life through Jesus Christ our Lord."

The BAD news: The consequences of sin is death. Death is not annihilation or ceasing to exist because we have an immortal soul. Death is "separation". Physical death results in a separation of the soul from the body. Spiritual death is a separation of the soul from God. Sin alienates mankind from his Creator.

Man does not naturally seek God's will or God's plan for his life. He seeks the fulfillment of his carnal and sinful desires. Phrased another way, the natural man is not even tuned in on God's frequency ... so how can he expect to discover and experience God's plan for his life? Man is all wrapped up in doing it "his own way."

The GOOD news: God's gift is eternal life through Jesus Christ. He reminds us in Romans 5:8, "But God commended his love toward us, in that, while we were yet sinners, Christ died for us." Or as John 3:16 phrases it: "For God so loved the world, that he gave his only begotten Son, that whosoever believeth in him should not perish, but have everlasting life."

God gives us the invitation to repent (turn from insisting on doing it our own way) and through faith, accepting God's gift of eternal life by receiving His Son as our personal Savior. Everything changes when one gets "saved."

The condemned sinner is now justified by faith in Christ. The sentence of death is commuted ... and the formerly condemned sinner is now pardoned.

Receiving Christ as one's Savior also results in being "born again" ... being reborn spiritually ... so that one is now tuned in on God's frequency and can begin discovering God's plan for his life.

In that same moment, one's relationship is changed ... from being a rebellious enemy of God ... to being adopted as a child of God. John 1:12 affirms it this way: "But as many as received him, to them gave he power to become the sons of God, even to them that believe on his name."

Bill had experienced that transformation back in Ohio and had made a good start. However, remember that his wife resented it deeply and gave him strong opposition. Then, when they moved to California, he did not establish a relationship with a vibrant local church.

Instead, on Sundays he drove the wife and in-laws around seeing the sights of Southern California. Bill's heart became cold, and as he phrased it: "I backslid," ... living with guilt and experiencing its consequences ... while at the same time ... being a victim of circumstances.

But there is more GOOD news. Isaiah 55:6-7 declares: "Seek ye the Lord while he may be found, call ye upon him while he is near: Let the wicked forsake his way, and the unrighteous man his thoughts: and let him return unto the Lord, and he will have mercy upon him; and to our God, for he will abundantly pardon."

Bill and Pat discovered that day ... that in spite of their past failures, it's OK ... you can "return"... you can come back home to the Lord. Mercy is another chance, even when we don't deserve another chance. Being abundantly pardoned is as good as it can get. Yes, there is "Hope For Wounded Warriors!!!"

In the rest of this book, Bill describes his personal journey with the Lord. Yours will be uniquely different ... but let me say that the best thing about having bi-focals and hearing aids ... is that we have lived long enough to see God's promises both vindicated and validated. Go for it!]

Bill continues: One thing I forgot to mention in the divorce, my attorney was in cahoots with the attorney that my "ex" had, and they worked against me in favor of her. I think the judge knew them both very well. Every time I opened my mouth to tell the judge something, he told me to shut up ... I was robbing her youth. Any man who would stay with a woman for 33 years was robbing her youth and didn't deserve a day in court, so he gave her everything.

He gave her all my books. The only thing I walked away with were the clothes on my back. He said that I had to give her a pension, half of my retirement for the rest of my life, and when I died, she would get a widow's pension. That was 27 years ago. Up to today, I still send her a check each month. I started at $300 but now with the cost of living increases, it's $883 each month. I have never missed a payment.

Getting back to my life with Patricia, the day we were married we received a couple thousand dollars in cash, so we went out house hunting. We went to Upland. There was one house left for sale in a new development near a railroad track. There was a high, twelve foot block wall. Only a couple of trains a day would pass through ... one was a passenger train in the morning, and one was a passenger train at night, plus a couple of freight trains, one going each way.

We didn't seem to mind the noise too bad, so we asked what we could buy it for, and he said, "49-9" ($49,900). It had four bedrooms ... actually 3 bedrooms and a den, a large family room, a large kitchen, a large formal dining room, and a large living room. Also, it had a study. It was a beautiful home. Later, we put in a swimming pool in the back.

Well, we hadn't started going to church yet, so I told Patricia that now that we had come back to the Lord, we needed to find a church. So I said, "Why don't we go to such-in-such church and see whether we like it there?"

Patricia had some Quaker background where people go to church and sit quietly and meditate. She had never been to a Pentecostal type service, but she said, "Alright. I don't know anything about them or anything about their religion, but we'll go and find out."

That Sunday night there was a service, and we went. It happened to be a night where Pentecostals might say that the Spirit was really moving among the people. Folks were running up and down the aisles, waving handkerchiefs, praising the Lord, screaming and yelling, and rolling in the aisles. It was a very demonstrative type church, and it scared Patricia very badly.

She started to slip down and slide forward on her seat. The first thing you know, she was sitting on the floor with her feet underneath the pews in front of her. She had her hands over her ears, and she looked wild-eyed. She grabbed me by the hand and said, "Get me out of here. These people have gone crazy."

So I helped her up, and we slipped out of the church. She said, "Don't you ever take me to a full gospel church again ... not like this one anyway." So I said, "Okay, we'll go to a more formal church."

Down the street, about four blocks from where we lived, was a Church of the Nazarene. I didn't know anything about the Nazarenes and neither did she, but we were church shopping, so that Sunday morning, we went. It was a wonderful service. In those days we sang hymns, and we had an organ, a piano, and a choir. The church was full. The pastor was a real gentle soul. That was the turning point in my life.

We were there for a couple years, and I started attending prayer meeting on Wednesday mornings, my day off. It was mostly retired folks that were attending. Of course, I was only in my early 50's then.

Among the group was a retired evangelist and architect ... he had drawn plans for over fifty churches in California. He said to me, "You know, it seems to me that you know the Bible very well ... and not only that, it seems to me that you have a special aura around you that tells me that you're not just an average layman."

I confessed, "Well, I guess you're right. I was a minister at one time." He said, "I thought so. Why are you out of the ministry?" And I said, "It's a long story, and I don't think I'll go into it ... but I don't think I'm worthy of going into the ministry again. I've had a divorce and a remarriage."

He said, "Well, what were the circumstances?" So I told him, and he said, "I don't think there is a whole lot against you." Well, I said, "The Lord hasn't called me back yet. He's just called me back to be a good Christian layman and that's what I intend to do.

So every Wednesday morning after prayer meeting, we would go to breakfast. He kept on, and then another member of the group, got on my case. He kept pushing me to go to the district and apply for a minister's license. I didn't want to do that. I said, "No, no, I don't want to do that." Well, the Lord began to speak to my heart, and I'd start crying as soon as I got inside the church. Then I would go down to the altar and start crying while I was praying.

Finally, Pat got fed up with it and said, "What you need to do is make a decision. You're either going to do what God wants you to do, or we can't make it together ... because I can't stand you breaking into tears every time we go to church.

So I said, "Okay," and the next Sunday night, after church, I made a commitment at the altar that I would look into getting a minister's license. It was scary. The future was unknown. But that simple act of obedience ... doing what I knew God wanted me to do, was a turning point in my life.

CHAPTER 11:
PALM SPRINGS –
THE IMPOSSIBLE DREAM

There was a small congregation of about 40 people in Palm Springs that had been meeting in a hotel basement room every Sunday for about ten years. Then the hotel took their room away from them as they needed it for storage.

So the group rented a storeroom, next to a bird sanctuary where they had all kinds of exotic birds, canaries, and parakeets. The birds were right next door, and the cockroach situation was desperate ... it was terrible. The place was overrun with them because of the birds.

The pastor who was there had a heart attack, and he was leaving this group. They had no pastor and many of them went elsewhere at that time, except five older couples. Two of them were quite wealthy, and the other three were just retired.

When they heard that I was a newly licensed minister, the retiring pastor called me up one day and asked me if I would pastor that church. I said, "Maybe ... I don't know if I can handle it." After all, I was a full time furniture salesman who was just beginning my first year of practical training.

He said, "Well, there are only ten people ... and our storeroom will only hold about 35 at the most. In the back there is a tiny 2x4 office for you. There's one room in the back that will hold a Sunday School class, and coffee and refreshments after church."

So I said, "Sure, I'll take it," but the church had not gone through the D.S. (District Superintendent ... whose function is to guide each church in the selection of their pastor.) There is a prescribed protocol for making pastoral arrangements, and we had by-passed the chain-of-command.

All military personnel know that chain-of-command is important ... and by-passing it can get you in big trouble. So on Monday I phoned the D.S., and said, "I've been asked to pastor the Palm Springs Church. What do you think about that?" He said, "Absolutely not! ... Absolutely not!" So I asked, "What's your reason?"

He explained that that church ... a tiny diminishing group of renegades meeting in a storeroom next to a bird sanctuary ... were an embarrassment to him. They hadn't paid their assigned budget shares for others, and they were ignoring the SOP (Standard Operating Procedures) for calling a pastor. It was his intentions to close that work. He gave me thirty days to rent a storage locker for the piano and other furnishings and instructions to bring him the bill for reimbursement.

I wasn't sure what to do. I really did not feel in my heart that this is what the Lord wanted me to do. So I preached for four Sundays. During that time the District Superintendent came down on a week night and talked to the ten people and told them what he was going to do.

He was right about them being a bunch of renegades. They objected. In fact, they tried to drown him out. They were trying to shout him down in what he was saying. He demanded order. He even took off his shoe, pounded it on the desk and said, "Order! Order! I want the attention of everyone here. This church is now closed officially. Pastor Lentsch is going to store all the stuff for the district, and you people can find other churches to gather in," ... and out he walked.

Well, five of the couples that were there came to me the following Wednesday night at prayer meeting and they asked, "How can we change his mind? We want you as our pastor. We like your preaching. You have preached four Sundays, and we want you to stay."

So I said, "I would suggest each family write him a letter and explain to him the reasons why you want to keep the church open and see what he says." So they sat down and each one wrote their letter.

He got all five letters, and he called me. He said, "What are you doing down there? I told you to close that church ... not to keep it open." I said, "I just don't feel comfortable closing this work." He said, "You don't have any say in it. I'm the D.S. I'm the one who has to make this decision, and I'm going to close that church."

So I asked, "Won't you give me at least six months to prove to you that you're wrong? At least be fair to me if not to these people." I said, "Give me an opportunity. If the church doesn't grow in six months, I'll close it."

"All right," he said, "I'll give you six months. But," he said, "in that six months I want you to have at least two new people who receive Christ as Savior, and I want all the budgets paid in full." He said, "They owe on their Educational Budget; they owe on the Missionary Budget; they owe on their District Budget. I want them all paid ... in full." So I said, "Okay, we'll take care of that."

The group had some funds in a savings account. I told them what the D.S. told me, so they sent a check to pay all those budgets in full for the year. But there remained the problem ... where was I going to find two people who needed the Lord to give their hearts to Him?

The first full Sunday, after all of this fell out, happened to be Easter Sunday. I tell you ... we had a full house. We had thirty inside that little storeroom and about twenty sitting outside. Of course, all of the people that come down from Canada and Washington and Oregon had come down in their campers to vacation in the Palm Springs area. At that time prices were not too high for campers and trailers.

Those folks came and helped to fill up the place. We had a special vocalist sing that day. It was a wonderful service. Two fourteen year old boys responded to the invitation and gave their hearts to Jesus. That was really encouraging for a brand new bi-vocational pastor in his first church.

Gleefully I phoned the District Superintendent. I said, "Doc, all the budgets are paid, and we had two teen boys who gave their hearts to Christ on Easter Sunday." "Okay, that's the first month. For the second month I want two more people saved and I want a letter from you stating how many people attended and how the offerings are going." I said, "Okay, I'll do that."

The next Sunday we had almost 50 people again because the snowbirds were still in the area. They didn't leave until May. We had a great service. At that particular time, a couple had an organ they wanted to sell, so they sold it to the church for $1500. I put in my share along with everybody else. Now, we had both a piano and an organ ... plus someone to play it.

The next Sunday, a young couple who lived in Redlands came and visited our service. They had come up to Palm Springs to stay in a hotel for the weekend. When the altar call was given, they came forward to give their hearts to the Lord. They were very happy with the church and with the group, so they asked for membership.

We had a problem. I couldn't officially receive anybody into membership yet. I was just an interim pastor. I was there because the D.S. said I could be there. He said he wouldn't appoint me until he was thoroughly satisfied that this church was going to amount to something.

So I said, "Wonderful," and I called the D.S. on Monday and told him we had received a good offering ... enough to cover expenses, and that we had two more folks who had accepted Christ's invitation as Savior and wanting to be received into membership. He said, "That's unbelievable. That's four in two weeks. I don't know what to say. You've still got three or four months left on your six months."

I know that it is hard in the summer to hold people in the desert. It gets hot and people leave ... and we didn't have too many local people yet who were attending. So I did a lot of hard praying in those days, and I told the Lord that if He wanted this work to succeed, He would have to help me find and attract new people. So we did some advertising in the newspaper.

One Sunday a man stopped by and visited the service. Afterwards, he came up to me and said he owned the radio station in Palm Springs. He was very impressed with the service and wanted to know if we were ever going to build a church facility. I said, "Oh yes. There are five couples here that own five lots all in a block over in Cathedral City. We are thinking about building the church there once I get my appointment by the district."

The District Superintendent had said they would carry us through the summer, but they wanted to see more people with transformed lives. They wanted a written report as to what we've done; what has been accomplished in this work at the end of the six months; how much we've taken in; and the whole enchilada so to speak. So when September came, I wrote him a full report, and he came down to formally appoint me as pastor.

Well, now I was officially appointed as a bi-vocational pastor, but still living in Upland and working in the furniture store. Pat and I drove down to Palm Springs every Wednesday afternoon after work and held the prayer meeting. Actually, while I wanted to get experience as a pastor, I didn't really like the desert. I didn't want to go to the desert.

Even my own pastor had said, "It's like taking a rattlesnake by the tail." But when God calls you to a ministry ... or to any other vocation in life, whatever that may be ... the best thing a person can do ... is obey. Do what you understand is God's direction for the next step ... and then trust Him for the resources and the details.

(At this point, Bill shares some of his difficult circumstances ... along with some very unique and personal "conversations" with God. The reader has to smile, as like the Psalmist in the Bible, Bill tells God his gut feelings ... which can be easily influenced by a bad case of self-pity.)

The distance was 150 miles round trip on Wednesday, and 150 miles round trip on Sunday. We had to lay over between services, so we wound up buying an old trailer that had been abandoned and deeded to this mobile home park. We bought it for $10,000 and moved in for Sundays, not realizing that one day it would be our home.

Well, as it was, I didn't want to move down there, but God had other ideas. So He began to deal with me about selling the house and moving down there, but I didn't want to do that. You know ... stubborn ... bullheaded. ... so God had to take me down a peg.

First thing I knew, my ulcerated colitis had started bleeding. It was really profuse. The doctor said they couldn't operate because it was too close to the end of the bowel system. He would have to put me on drugs plus strained baby food. At the time, it seemed like the Lord was whispering in my mind, "This is just the beginning." So as I began to suffer with the pain and agony, Pat came home and said she had lost her job.

Meanwhile, I was a General Manager in a large furniture store in Upland. I did all the hiring, firing, advertising, did a little bit of everything. I was very contented until one of the owners passed away. The other owner came to me and said, "We want our son to be manager. You can go back to sales."

I wasn't too happy with that, but I was willing to accept it. Then he added, "You'll work Sundays." Well I didn't want to work Sundays because I was pastoring down at Palm Springs, so I told him, "I can't work on Sundays. I have a church to run." He says, "Well, make a choice. It's either us or them." So, while it was scary walking away from a job, I made my choice and left.

So then I went to the unemployment bureau to collect unemployment insurance or to find another job. They told me that if I didn't work on Sundays in the furniture business, then they couldn't find me work. I wasn't eligible. So you notice how the Lord was closing doors one after another.

Without a job ... and Pat without a job ... and me going through the physical suffering and pain of what was happening to me internally, God spoke to me gently and said, "Put your house up for sale and move to Palm Springs." I said, "No, Lord, I don't really want to do that. I'll commute like I've been doing."

Well then, Pat came down with Bell's palsy. That's a debilitating disease where your eye droops and your mouth droops ... and you drool ... and your speech is impaired to a certain degree ... and you're miserable ... and it seemed to me God was saying, "This is only the beginning. You go to Palm Springs. Put your house up for sale." Again I said 'No, Lord, I really don't want to."

The next morning I felt impressed to go into my study. As I went in and sat down, the Lord spoke to my heart and said, "Close your eyes. I want to show you something." At that moment I felt the presence of a person on one side of me and another on the other side. The one on the right side said, "How can you serve a God like this? He took your jobs away. He has allowed illness upon both you and your wife. Why are you being so faithful to Him when all of these things are coming on you?"

Then the presence on the left side, "Rebuke him. That is Satan. Rebuke him in the name of Jesus," ... which I did. Then that negative presence left me. Then the Lord said, "I'm going to show you ... if you don't take this church and build it for me ... what the end results will be."

A large screen came up ... it was huge and it just covered the whole of one wall. A man was smiling at the edge of the screen and the Lord asked, "You recognize him?" I said, "Yes, that's my friend, Fred. He just passed away a couple of weeks ago. I was at his funeral." Well he said, "He's here with me and that's why I want you to go to Palm Springs. One day you'll be here smiling too."

In the background were thousands of people. I couldn't distinguish who they were, but I had an idea that there were a lot of them that I knew. He whispered in my heart, "These are the souls who will not be won to me if you don't go to Palm Springs as I have asked you to do. Think about it for a moment before you say 'No,' again."

Then I thought about it and thought, well, I'm being unfair to those people because they'll never find Jesus without me going ... then I should go. So I said, "Alright, Lord, you've convinced me."

Then the Lord said to me in my mind ... "I will heal you within a month after you have gone to Palm Springs. I will heal you completely. Then three weeks later lay hands upon your wife and anoint her, and have everyone in the congregation gather around and I will heal her." So I said, "Alright, Lord."

So the next day we listed our house ... and mind you now, there were about eight houses in this tract that were up for sale ... the only difference between those houses and ours, was that our house was on the railroad track

We listed the house one day, and the next day a lady that Pat had worked with at Wards called her and said, "I see your house is listed. Can we buy it?" Pat said, "Well, we listed it at $108,000. If you want to pay that, that's fine." So she said, "We want the house, don't sell it."

She came out that night with her husband and children, and they looked it over, and were satisfied that this was the house they wanted to buy. We told them about the train, but they still wanted to buy it at $108,000.

When they went to escrow the lender would only loan $103,000 on the house. So that left her $5000 short. She told us that she was having a time because she didn't have enough money down, but not to sell it. She wanted it, so she got a $5000 loan from her father, and they bought the house with a 30 day escrow.

Meanwhile, we got a couple of young men from the church and a U-Haul truck. They loaded everything but our clothes and kitchen utensils. Some of it went into the mobile home, but most of it was put in one of the storage facilities in Cathedral City. So we moved into the trailer in the mobile home park not very far from the church property.

Then the Lord began to show me His plan. We were holding services and having great success all winter long. We had people sitting outside with the doors and windows open ... sitting in lawn chairs. It was a great time of fellowship and worship. God was just blessing.

He spoke to me and said, "You have $1000 in an account. I want you to put that $1000 in a check up on the pulpit, and I want you to challenge the people to match it. I want you to start raising money because you're going to build a church."

That next Sunday morning, we had a packed house ... as many as 35 inside and probably 20-25 outside. They were sitting in lawn chairs. We had a PA system so they could hear. I said to them, "God has instructed me to take a $1000 and challenge you to meet that for our new building. Five lots all together have been donated. We're going down to the land title company, have them made into one parcel, and we'll break ground as soon as we get some plans approved to build a church."

Well, we raised about $30,000 that Sunday. Of course, that's not nearly enough, so about a month later the Lord says to me, "You have a $1000 in your savings account. Take that out and challenge the people again." So I did, and I took the $1000 ... but I hated to do it as we had no jobs and the church was just paying me $50 a week. I just hated to take what little money we had in case of an emergency. But the Lord said, "Trust me." So I did, and we challenged them. That took the amount up to $89,000. So now we were sitting on $89,000 in pledges and cash.

Now the Lord said, "You go back to Upland and talk to George, that retired architect. He has drawn plans for 50 churches. He is well equipped to draw plans for this church. You tell him what you want, and he'll do it."

So I went to the Upland prayer meeting that next Wednesday morning, and at breakfast I said, "George, the Lord has been dealing with me for you to draw blueprints for our church." He says, "Oh. No. I'm retired. I'm through drawing blueprints." I said, "George, the Lord has spoken to me to speak to you." George responded, "Well, He hasn't said anything to me and I don't think I want to do it." So I said, "Well, okay, that's fine. I don't want to keep pestering you by phone, but I'll be down here next week for prayer meeting and breakfast with you until you consent."

The next week I went for breakfast and buttonholed him again about it. Finally, he said, "Alright, I'll draw plans for your church." So we sat down together, and I told him basically what we wanted, what size, and how much money we had to work with.

George knew that a God-given vision attracts resources. Even in the midst of the Great Depression, men dreamed about and constructed that awesome Golden Gate Bridge. George also knew that without a plan, a vision is only a fantasy. Put another way, if you don't have a plan ... you

125

don't really have a project. You need a plan in order to communicate and inspire others to participate. So he said, "Okay, I'll draw the plans and get them approved."

They were beautiful plans, and we put them on the wall of our rented storeroom church ... hoping to communicate the vision. Offerings were still coming in from Oregon and Washington, Idaho and Indiana. It came from everywhere as we began to gather in that $89,000. So now, here we had the plans.

One of our wealthy starters from the beginning of the work, a fellow by the name of Gus, owned a business, an electrical business up in northern California. He happened to be in one of his cottages on a lake, and I called him and told him we had the plans. So he says, "Send the plans up, and let me look at them."

I rolled a copy of the plans up, put them in a tube, and mailed them to him. He called me long distance when they came. He said, "I looked the plans over. They seem OK to me. Go ahead and start looking. Call the Young brothers down there in Indio, and you tell them you want them to come up with a backhoe and dig the foundations for the church."

"In the meanwhile, let me know the date. I'll get a hold of that Hispanic gardener and his workers and tell them to meet at the grounds that same day so they can make the forms for the foundation."

We called the Mayor of Cathedral City and all the officials and the newspaper. They all came out on a certain Saturday, and they took their shovels and each one stuck it in the ground for the newspaper photographer ... and we were on our way.

Now I know that $89,000 isn't enough to build the beautiful edifice that God gave us to build. We lacked funds, so I called the District Superintendent. I said, "Doc, I need an $80,000 loan from the District." (Here's where respecting the chain-of-command paid off.)

There was a long silence. Finally he says, "I told you, Bill, I don't want you to build a church in Palm Springs. These people ... I'm tired of problems with them. I told you I wanted you to store the furniture. Instead you talked me into appointing you as an interim pastor ... and now you've got about 50 members. But," he said, "I'll pray about it."

Soon after, there was a luncheon in Upland, some kind of a district event, and I went. I cornered him again and I said, "I'm still waiting for that $80,000 loan." He said, "I'll get back to you later this week." He called me and said, "We'll loan it to you on one condition. How much money do you have?" I said, "About $90,000" He said, "Alright, I don't think you can build this church with $170,000, but I'm willing to go along with you because God seems to be in it."

Well, things really began to happen. They dug and poured the foundation and slab. They put in the sewer lines ... the water lines ... the electrical lines. Then they started to frame the building.

After we got it framed, the Young brothers came back with a crane, and they lifted the sealed laminated beams into the top of the building. We had four big beams to put across the top of the church to anchor the sides, front, and the back. We were progressing.

(I confess, I was tempted to leave out the next few pages from Bill's original story. Most readers might not be interested in the details. But the lessons here are important.

Every time Bill faced a challenge – roof – carpet – furnishings – plumbing – landscaping – he would pray about it … and God would send someone as an answer. Bill had learned that if you are in a place of obedience to God, you can apply God's promises to your everyday life. The Bible, in Philippians chapter 4, can be paraphrased:

- Don't worry about anything.
- Do pray about everything.
- Tell God your needs.
- And don't forget to thank Him for His answers to your prayers.
- If you do this, the peace of God that passes all understanding will keep your hearts and minds through Christ Jesus.)

The plans called for a rustic stone front to the church with a large stained glass window. All the windows were stained glass on the side of the church that faced the road. The other side was a solid wall because of the fellowship hall and offices.

We prayed about it, and the Lord came through. We had money donated for the stained glass window in the front. People from the Upland church gave enough money to get the other five side stained glass windows put in. The one in the front was a beautiful picture of our Lord.

We found a stone mason over in Desert Hot Springs. He came, and looked it over. He said, "I think I can do that. I'll donate my labor, but you have to buy the rustic stones." So we bought all the stones needed … pieces of rock … and he did a beautiful job on the front of the church.

After we came to the point of putting the roof on … they had put the plywood sheets on, someone said they needed money. A fellow called me and said that he would donate the funds for the roof ... not to worry about it. He sent me a check for $5000. So that put the roof on.

After we got the roof on, we started on the plaster board. Then we needed paint. Gus knew this man that was attending the Indio church in the winter months. He was a snowbird, and he owned a paint factory up in Idaho, so Gus called him. He responded, "Just tell me how much paint you need and what color you need, and I'll bring it down to you the next time I come down." Gus said, "Fine." So we had paint to paint the walls on the inside and tape to tape them.

Now we lacked carpet. We lacked a pulpit. We lacked pews and altar benches. But the Lord was with us, and He spoke to hearts. We got a telephone call from a couple who lived in Bend, Oregon. They said to meet them over at Gus's house where they were vacationing. They would like to talk about furnishing the carpets in the church and would also talk about the pews ... that they would furnish them as well. So I went over and had lunch at Gus's house while they were there. We ordered the oak pews and soon the carpet arrived by freight from Georgia.

Now we needed the pulpit, communion table and prayer benches. We didn't have them, but someone said that there is a fellow in the Upland church that does marvelous woodworking. We had $1300 in our special memorial fund that people had put in there in lieu of flowers at funerals. They gave permission to take that money and have him make the pulpit, communion table, and altar.

So I called this man, and he said, "Yes, I can buy the materials for the $1300 but that would leave nothing for labor. My labor comes high because I'm a cabinet maker, and I make good money." I said, "We'll pray about it. Maybe the Lord will have you do it for us."

About a week went by, and we were progressing on the church. The telephone rang and he said, "I'll do it. I'll give it to the Lord, my services. Can you meet me at the Upland Church this Monday, and we can set it up. I have some plans I can show you, and you can pick out the ones you want, and how you want them built. I'll build them and deliver them when they are finished. "

So the Lord's work was moving right along. We needed a refrigerator, and the Lord spoke to me, so Pat and I bought a nice refrigerator for the fellowship hall. Then we had the plumbing problem. We had no money to put fixtures in the Ladies Room or the Men's Room ... nor the money to lay the tile. We didn't even have the tile for the floors.

I did a lot of hard praying, and finally someone said to Gus, "I'm a plumber and I heard you need fixtures for two bathrooms. I'll go ahead and foot the bill. I'll install them and give it to the Lord." So he went in and installed the fixtures.

Then John, a Catholic fellow who had come to the Lord ... his wife was a backslidden Nazarene ... they both gave their hearts to Christ. He was a tile man and he came in and tiled the floors in both restrooms so we got those done. He donated both the tile and the labor.

Now we were just about complete except we didn't have any lighting fixtures in the church. Gus, being a lighting expert, he called his son up in a community around Walnut. His son said, "Yup, Dad, I can ship those fixtures down" So Gus bought the fixtures and installed the lighting system. He installed the PA system that was given to us by the owner of the radio station down there in Palm Springs. So we were pretty much ready to go.

But we didn't have any landscaping. Nor did we have the sidewalks or the curbing. The parking lot was not in either. We had the money to do most of this, so Gus went out shopping, and we bought the light standards to go up in the parking lot. We got them put in, and then we had to get the blacktop. It was about 115 degrees the day we got the blacktop. They poured that asphalt and rolled it out.

One of the men in the church and I spent most of the afternoon with a pickax cutting out the excess blacktop around the light standards because we wanted to make sure there was plenty of space in case they wanted to put flowers around them. It was very hot, and the blacktop was very hot.

I spent many hours with pick and shovel digging trenches for water lines. We got those water lines in and ready to be hooked up to the city system. Meanwhile Gus and I pulled light wires from each of the parking lot standards through an underground tube into the church's electrical panel.

Now, everything was done except the landscaping ... but wouldn't you know? We ran out of money. So I went to the landscapers. The owner had been in a terrible auto accident. The family had called me to go visit him and pray with him, and so I did. This was before the church was built when we were in the storeroom church. So I decided to call him to landscape the place.

I called him and told him who I was, and he said, "Oh, yeah. You're the guy who came out and prayed for me at the hospital. I appreciated that." I said, "I need a favor in the landscaping. I need three or four palm trees and a half dozen

Jacaranda trees, and we need grass. We need to have it in by Friday of this week."

This was a Monday when I called him. He says, "Have you got the money? I've made a note of what you need. The job is going to cost you between five and six thousand dollars." I said, "No, but we're good for it." He says, "No, I've got to have a check in hand before I can do anything."

So again I got on my knees and began to pray, "Lord, we've sent out three hundred notices to pastors and churches that we are going to have open house and dinner on the grounds, and the District Superintendent was coming to dedicate the church. Lord, we need it done for Sunday, or we can't open the doors."

I really knew the Lord was going to have to send money, so I got off my knees and sat at my desk with my head in my hands ... and asking the Lord, "I don't know what we are going to do. We're in a bind. We can't hold services until we get approval from the city, and they won't approve it until all the landscaping is in. What will we do?"

A thought came into my mind ... call Cloris at the Upland Church and tell her your plight. She knows how to pray. So I picked up the phone, and called her. Cloris said, "Well, I'll get back to you in about an hour." In about an hour, she called and asked how much did we need? I said that I thought about $5000 would cover it. She said, "There'll be a check in the mail for $5000." I said, "I need it quicker. I got to have it here by Friday." She said, "It'll be there by Friday, don't worry, I'll put it in the mail today. This is only Monday and you'll get it."

So I called the landscaper and told him there would be a check in the mail for me by Friday. He said, "Alright, on your word as a pastor that I'll get paid when the job's done." So he went ahead and put in the trees and shrubs and sowed the grass. Then he sprayed it green. It was about 5:00 o'clock on Friday when the check arrived by registered mail ... and I endorsed it over to him.

As he was about to pull away, I said, "Wait a minute. We need to get final approval on this. It's pretty late. I don't know if I can get final approval, but we're scheduled to have service on Sunday." So he says, "Wait a minute, I'll call the City Manager."

He got on the telephone and called the city. They said the City Manager was just about to leave, so he says, "Put him on the line, I need to talk to him." The landscaper said, "Joe, I want you to come out to the brand new church on Cathedral Drive and do a final inspection so they can have services Sunday." "Oh," the City Manager says, "I'll do it on Monday. Tell them they can wait."

He said, "Joe, I got to have this done today. They can't have services on Sunday unless you give the final approval. Why don't you swing by on your way home ... you'll be driving up Cathedral Drive. Do a run through and give it your approval?" He continued, "You know, you owe me a lot of favors because I've done lots of favors for the city. I'm calling in some of those favors." So the City Manager says, "OK, I'll drop by."

You have got to know: Friends are for when you need them! That landscaper saved the day ... and the whole weekend.

In about 10 minutes the City Manager drove up. The church was open. I was standing out in the parking lot. He came up and looked at me and says, "Are you the pastor?" I said, "Yes." He came in, and I pointed out to him the carpets and the whole bit, the paint and everything we had done, and he says, "Beautiful job. Beautiful job. I approve and you can hold services on Sunday." I said, "Can I have a written statement to that effect in case the police come by? He says, "Oh, no. Just tell the police if they come by and give you any trouble to call the City Manager at home. They have my number." "OK, " so the landscaper left smiling.

He was happy, and I was happy because the church was ready, and Sunday afternoon at 2:00 o'clock, we held services. The District Superintendent came out. He hadn't seen the church ... only when it was first framed.

He was so impressed he said, "I can't believe that you did this. I don't believe that God did this, I really don't. It's a miracle. You have really done it!" I said, "I've done it because I have blind faith. I trusted the Lord. He spoke to my heart, and He told me what to do, and I did it. ... and this is why."

He asked, "How much of a mortgage have you got on this church?" I said, "Well, we just owe you people, the District, that's all. We'll make the payments on time. You can count on that." He responded, "That's wonderful. You mean you built this church for $170,000?" I said, "Yes, sir, all the rest was donated materials, donated labor, and with God's help, it's done."

All through the construction I did a lot of sweeping of bits of wood and sawdust and dirt. When it came to the manual labor, I helped pull the electrical wires through the conduits and did a lot of work, but I was thrilled to be able to be a part of that project and help build that church.

Sunday afternoon cars began to roll in. We had spaces all marked off. The blacktop man had come back and put in the parking lines. The place was full, and some were sitting in lawn chairs outside the church.

We shared testimonies of praise ... recounting all of the awesome ways that God had answered our prayers. Then the District Superintendent dedicated the church ... preaching a sermon on church dedication and calling it "The Miracle Church."

I served in the Palm Springs church for five years. We built a house; put in a swimming pool and had a nice front lawn part of the time, ... when the wind wasn't blowing and filling it up full of big sand dunes. But it was a nice house.

We saw it from the plans, and they built it for us ... and God really blessed us while we were there for those five years. The congregation grew and paid on the indebtedness as promised. Things were really humming along.

One Sunday, I was preaching in an evening service, and the Lord spoke to me before the prayer time that I would be leaving this church and that I should pray about it. Next morning I was a little shook up. I went into the church early ... knelt at the altar, and I asked the Lord just what He wanted me to do. An inner voice just said, "You'll leave this church within six months. Put in for another church. Your work here is done."

It was hard for me. Most of these people came in under my ministry, other than the ten we started with. We were running now close to 100. I had a lot of deep feelings because of all the work we put in on the church ... the hours, the sweat, and tears and prayers that went into building this work. It was hard to leave. But I really felt strongly that I should leave.

I told Patricia about my decision to resign from the Palms Springs pastorate. It was hard to convince her that this was the will of God because she had gotten a good job. It was a miracle that she got the job. I remember when we were in the mobile home living on $50 a week ... $200 a month, and we were praying that God would help her find work.

One day she saw an ad in the newspaper that said that a local bank was looking for tellers. So she said, "Well, I can try to get that job." She went over and applied. They said, "To be honest with you, we wanted a younger person on the window because it's proven out that in this area it's all elderly people and they want a young face ... but we will keep your application on file and if another job opens up in the bank, we'll call you."

About a week later she got a call ... this time from one of their branches. She went in for an interview ... took a typing test and passed it. So the bank manager told her, "What your job will be is to take care of the safety deposit boxes, and you'll be typing letters for me as my assistant and doing odd jobs around, taking the place of tellers that are off sick. You'll be a utility person." That job was such a blessing. It all came about because of faith in God to supply all of our needs. (Philippians 4:19)

Believing it was time to leave, I called the District Superintendent, and I told him. He said, "Don't do anything. I'm coming out to visit with you." So he came out one night, and we had cake and coffee at the house.

He said, "Tell me about your wanting to leave." I explained it to him about how I felt and he said, "Are you sure this is God's will?" I said, "Well, I think it is. I'm not ... I have no way to be entirely positive. It's possible that I'm wrong, but I don't believe I am." So he says, "You pray about it for a couple weeks and then call me." So I said, "OK."

The D.S. and his wife had open house at their home in Santa Ana, so we went to the celebration. After everybody had left, I stayed about a half hour and talked with him and told him that I really, and truly felt that God had spoken to me telling me it was time to move on. So he said, "Bill, it's up to you if you want to give a thirty day notice to the church. Meanwhile, I'll try to find another pastor to take the church."

Bill and Pat moved on with life ... relocating in San Diego. They continued in ministry, taking assignments to hurting congregations and encouraging people to bring the broken pieces of life to God where they might experience the freedom of His forgiveness and His transforming power that brings hope for today and for the tomorrows.

In each of those assignments they faced the same kinds of "impossible" challenges. While the details changed ... the drill was basically the same:

1. Ascertain God's will.

2. Pray fervently.

3. Trust God's promises.

4. Be willing to work and sacrifice.

5. Celebrate God's awesome answers.

In 1998 Bill acknowledged that God began to lead him to retire. "I was now about 76 years old and was getting kind of weary of the day to day demands of pastoring ... but not from serving the Lord."

Following "retirement," Bill completed work on a Doctor of Ministry degree, taught part time in a Seminary, and served part-time on a church staff as a Pastor to Senior Adults. Bill turned 90 on May 13, 2012. He is experiencing challenges with cataracts, and has had to give up driving though he still leads Bible study groups.

CHAPTER 12: PATRICIA'S CANCER

Shortly after that retirement, Patricia came down with ovarian cancer. It was a strange cancer at that time in how it was discovered. She went to her doctor, and they took a pap smear. It looked irregular, so her doctor thought a hysterectomy was in order.

When they went in, they removed the part of the body that they thought was cancerous. They sent it to the lab during surgery and it came back benign. But they did find three other tumors which they removed. They sent her to chemotherapy as soon as she got out of the hospital.

In spite of being on chemotherapy, new tumors developed. They became very numerous. In fact the doctor said there were five major tumors on the second surgery two years later. That was a very serious four and a half hour operation. But the Lord brought her through all right. She went on chemo again ... trying to destroy the new tumors that had appeared.

I went through a very difficult time with the Lord during that time in between that surgery and the accompanying chemo. I asked the Lord, "Lord, you know that I have served you faithfully most of my life ... and I really and truly do not understand why You don't heal her and why You are allowing this to happen to her."

A Voice so clear to me just said, "I want you to remember that she is my child. She belongs to me. She doesn't belong to you. I have loaned her to you, and I can do whatever I want to do with her life. You must learn to live by faith and accept what happens as being in my will."

Then scripture came to mind, verses from Philippians chapter 4. Summarized it says: "Rejoice in the Lord always ... The Lord is at hand. Don't worry about anything but in everything by prayer and supplication, with thanksgiving; let your requests be made known to God, and the peace of God that passes all understanding will keep your hearts and minds in Christ Jesus."

That was the Scripture that the Lord gave me and that I have relied upon since. It has strengthened my faith. It has strengthened my resolve to continue working hard for Him and I will.

Meanwhile, it is my hope that by sharing "My Story" others ... especially those wounded warriors returning from Iraq and Afghanistan will take courage to trust the Lord and begin to discover and experience God's very best for their lives.

It all begins with that simple prayer of confession, together with faith in Jesus Christ. God is able to take the "mangled mess" of anyone's dysfunctional past and transform it into something beautiful.

AUTHOR'S EPILOGUE

After Bill had dictated that last chapter; Patricia survived various cycles of cancer treatments. Together they enjoyed precious years of retirement that included five cruises and trips to various parts of the USA before her final battle with cancer and her home-going on June, 11, 2009. Bill describes those years as a "bowl of cherries without the pits!"

We would acknowledge that in the last half of his life, Bill had a very unique personal relationship with the Lord. When describing his personal journey of seeking God's direction, he would often use the phrase, "So the Lord said to me ..." to communicate his perception of what he sensed to be God's will.

Hopefully the reader will not be spooked by such phrasing, but rather take heart, that with a close walk with the Lord, it is possible to discern God's direction in our daily lives and go forward with a quiet confidence in spite of outward circumstances.

If, like a football game, you divide Bill's life into four quarters, one sees the impact during the first quarter of a dysfunctional family and his desire to escape ... first by going to Georgia and then by joining the Marines.

The "second quarter" was filled with a lot of frustration, disappointment, and anger. It began with the feelings of helplessness and hopelessness ... accented with lots of pain ... as the Navy doctors did their best to save his shattered leg following his escape from the sinking USS Vincennes at Guadalcanal.

Then the ambiguities of seeking reemployment as a disabled wounded warrior haunted him at times. All of that was compounded with the bitterness that surrounds a dysfunctional marriage ... justifying some inappropriate escapades on his own part ... and finally prompting potentially disastrous thoughts of revenge ... including murder and suicide.

The "third quarter" really began when Bill and Patricia ... in desperation, acknowledged their need and as Bill phrases it: "Got back to the Lord." During that "third quarter" they began to discover and experience the awesomes that accompany a life dedicated to pleasing God and helping others.

They demonstrated downright "gutsy" faith ... and God honored that faith in some wonderful ways ... as they sought to salvage a dying church and build significant facilities for its future.

The last quarter has been marked by their continued passion for helping others to discover the freedom of forgiveness and the peace that passes all understanding as one develops his/her own personal relationship with God. The whole process testifies to the reality: There is "Hope for Wounded Warriors !"

Perhaps you identify with some of life's battles similar to those that Bill has fought:

- a childhood impacted by a dysfunctional family life
- some inappropriate personal choices (dumb stuff that brought negative consequences)
- decisions by others and circumstance over which you had no control.

Hope gets regenerated when one realizes that, in spite of the past, God has a future for us. That is "Good News" ... yet many are unaware of how to begin to discover and experience His plan.

The Bible pictures Jesus standing at the door knocking. He promises that if we will open the door, He will come in. Why not do it right now?

That is the first step. Now determine to follow Him. Like Bill, find a Bible believing church home where they will help you nurture that new spiritual life and where you can enjoy the fellowship of being part of the family of God.

Let's see what God wants to do ... in you ... for you ... and through you!

Larry J. Webb

HopeforWoundedWarriors@gmail.com

HOPE FOR WOUNDED WARRIORS

33377332R00088

Made in the USA
Charleston, SC
13 September 2014